THE DRAMA OF
THE SOVIET 1960s

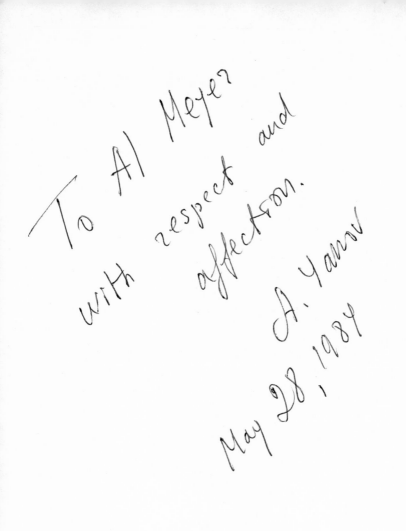

To Al Meyer
with respect and
affection.
A. Yanov
May 28, 1984

RESEARCH SERIES

No. 56

The Drama of the Soviet 1960s

A Lost Reform

ALEXANDER YANOV

INSTITUTE
OF INTERNATIONAL
STUDIES
University of California, Berkeley

Translated by Stephen P. Dunn

Library of Congress Cataloging in Publication Data

Yanov, Alexander.
    The drama of the Soviet 1960s.

    (Research series, ISSN 0068-6093; no. 56)
    Translated from Russian.
    Includes bibliography and index.
    1. Soviet Union—Rural conditions. 2. Soviet Union—
Social conditions—1945-   . 3. Peasantry—Soviet Union.
4. Soviet Union—Politics and government—1953-   .
I. Title. II. Series: Research series (University of Califor-
nia, Berkeley. Institute of International Studies); no. 56.
HN523.5.Y36 1984   306'.0947   84-6751
ISBN 0-87725-156-8

To the memory
of the great Russian reformer
Ivan Nikiforovich Khudenko

Two Russias face to face . . .

Anna Akhmatova

In the earlier period the West could safely
experiment with various assumptions about
the true nature of the Soviet regime, and how
it would or could be changed. The margin of
military safety was sufficient to take risks.
That is no longer the case.

William E. Odom

Timing points to the 1980s as a critical
decade, the first really dangerous decade since
the end of World War II.

Carl-Friedrich von Weizsacker

CONTENTS

Table of Contents

Acknowledgments

A number of generous organizations and institutions made it possible for me to work on this study throughout my years in Berkeley between 1978 and 1982: the National Endowment for the Humanities, the Earhart Foundation, the National Council for Soviet and East European Research, and the Institute of International Studies. Vera Dunham, Karin Beros, Gregory Grossman, Sidney Monas, George Breslauer, Carl Rosberg, Aron Katsenelinboigen, and Philip Siegelman were among the people who honored me with their friendship and gave me the moral support without which this book could not have been written. I want to use this opportunity to thank them all. I am also very grateful to Stephen P. Dunn, who translated a large part of this book into English with his usual brilliance.

A. Y.

Prologue

My original intentions in writing this book were quite ambitious. Its fundamental concept was based on the pattern of failed and reversed reforms—unique in European history—which have effectively precluded the political modernization of Russia up to the present day. This is not to say that there have been no successful reforms throughout the centuries of Russian history; none has been irreversible, however. The drama of Restoration (or counterreform) that England and France experienced only once in their history (respectively in 1660-1688 and 1814-1830) has been experienced by Russia over and over throughout its tortuous history—ever since it became an empire in the mid-sixteenth century.[1] It is this pattern that led me to suggest in an earlier work that reform versus counterreform—not reform versus revolution—constitutes the fundamental dichotomy of the Russian political process.

Not only is the Russian empire, according to this concept, different in its basic patterns of political change from any other member of the European family of nations, as well as from Oriental polities, but it seems to belong to a different age. Even now, near the end of the nuclear twentieth century, it remains essentially a medieval political system—playing in the modern world arena its ancient games according to its own idiosyncratic rules and taboos.

The principal distinction of the Russian political system (as I have tried to establish in a number of studies)[2] lies in the basic

[1] In the context of this study, the Russian Reform is defined as a set of socioeconomic and institutional changes moving the system in the direction of political modernization (whether or not they are so designed)—i.e., toward a polity in which political opposition is institutionalized as part of the normal functioning of the state. Accordingly a counterreform is defined as a set of policies and institutional changes related to the restoration of dictatorship and moving the system away from political modernization.

[2] See, for example, *The Origins of Autocracy: Ivan the Terrible in Russian History* (Berkeley: University of California Press, 1981), and *The Russian New*

heterogeneity of its political culture, in the fundamental, perhaps even ontological, dualism that has characterized it from its very inception—that is, from the time of the original clash and then uneasy symbiosis between the dynamic and reformist European culture of the Norsemen-founders of Kievan Rus' and the stagnant and dictatorial Byzantine political influences under which the state was formed at the end of the first Christian millennium.

For a long time, due perhaps to the disintegration of the Kievan state and the following centuries of the Tatar yoke, this dualism remained latent. It reemerged, however, in Muscovy in the middle of the fifteenth century—with the European component of the Russian equilibrium prevailing over its Byzantine rival. A century later, in the course of one of the greatest reforms in Russian history, that of the 1550s, the European component seemed to be winning the perennial struggle. It was then that the first and one of the most brutal of the Russian counterreforms reversed the process in a violent "revolution from above" of the 1560s led by Tsar Ivan IV, known to posterity as Ivan the Terrible.

And so it went for centuries after that: whenever a reform threatened to move Russia irreversibly toward political moderni-zation, a counterreform was there to reverse the process. In this sense the Bolshevik counterreform of October 1917, traditionally referred to as a great *revolution*, was no different from Ivan the Terrible's, which had no doubt also been a great revolution in terms of the institutional and ideological changes it introduced. Both revolutions destroyed the old regime, replacing it with a brutal garrison-state dictatorship; both arrested change toward political modernization; both institutionalized the counterreformist tendencies of the system. This comparison gives the reader the key to my conceptual frame-work: in Russia we seem to be dealing with a dynamic and self-perpetuating equilibrium in which the central theme of political history is the struggle of Russia versus Russia.

It was in this framework that I intended to reconstruct the story of the failure of a reformist attempt of the Soviet 1960s in which I took part. Rather than describe it in the conventional terms

Right (Berkeley: Institute of International Studies, 1978), as well as my essays "The Drama of the Time of Troubles," *Canadian-American Slavic Studies* 12, 1 (Spring 1978) and "Flight from Theory," *Slavic Review*, Summer 1983.

of Khrushchev's "erratic behavior" or of Khrushchev as an "embattled consumer advocate," as it is usually presented in sovietology, I intended to place this reform in the context of long-term historical patterns—in the context of the general phenomenon of Russian reform. From this changed angle of vision, a previously unexplored political universe seemed to open before me. If it is assumed that in analyzing recent Russian history we are dealing with a medieval political system for which communism is only one of many transitory socioeconomic and ideological forms, then the battle against "communist evil" on which the traditional or "totalitarian" (as I call it) school of thought in sovietology focuses seemed to lose much of its relevance. The chief rival of the totalitarianists—the "revisionist" school of thought which developed in reaction to their static, rigid depiction of Soviet reality—seemed to be no more relevant. Its attempt to apply to the analysis of a medieval system the methodologies currently in use in political science and derived from the experiences of modern Western polities (factional conflict theory or theories of bureaucratization, oligarchy, coalition-building, and political participation) succeeded only in giving the Russian empire an unrealistic modern and, in some cases, even Western cast. In addition, just as the totalitarianists do, the revisionists tend to see the Soviet state as a new nation born in 1917. Certainly there is no place for a pattern of failed and reversed reforms or for a Russian counterreform in either of their political universes.

In other words, just as the totalitarian theoretical model cannot account for the continual *emergence* of reforms pervading Russian (including Soviet) political history, so the revisionist theoretical models are not able to accommodate the continual *failure* of these reforms. We need to work out an alternative, post-revisionist theoretical model which, being based on the fundamental dualism of the Russian/Soviet system, can explain both the emergence of the reform of the 1920s (which followed the garrison-state dictatorship of 1918-1921) and the reversal of that reform in the 1930s by a counterreform as brutal as that of Ivan the Terrible. This is all the more necessary because in the second half of the twentieth century we are faced with the similar task of explaining both the emergence of the 1960s reform (which also followed a garrison-state dictatorship) and the fading away of that reform into a protracted regime of political stagnation. In this sense, the history of the 1960s reform was no different from that of its predecessors—the reforms of the 1600s, the 1720s, and the 1860s—all of which faded away into similar, Brezhnev-style regimes of political stagnation.

Thus it appears that even if everything else changed in the "new" nation, the *patterns of change* did not. And judging from the previous cases of political stagnation, the current regime can delay for only a few years or decades a desperate new reformist attempt, such as those of the 1680s, the 1820s, the early 1880s, and February 1917, and then, if it fails (as all similar attempts have), a new Russian counterreform will follow.

*   *

Why have all the reforms failed? In terms of my conceptual framework, this is the most important question facing the Russian historian or sovietologist. This is especially so if the emergence of a new Russian counterreform, which could be disastrous in the nuclear age both for Russia and for the world, is contingent on the success or failure of a new reformist attempt. If that is the case, then an analysis of the causes of the previous failures might be considered an urgent political problem. Here theory intertwines with politics, and the question of why all Russian reformist leaders, beginning with Aleksei Adashev in the mid-sixteenth century to the hapless Petr Stolypin, Vladimir Lenin (the revolutionary-turned-reformer after 1921), Nikolai Bukharin, and Nikita Khrushchev in the twentieth, were defeated assumes a paramount practical importance.

However it may be, this is what I tried to find out. Were their defeats inevitable, or were they due to some persistent pattern of political error committed by all these leaders? If there is such a pattern, can it be formulated? Can a hypothetical model of a Russian reform attempt be derived from such analyses? Can we determine the basic prerequisites for the success of a reform? These are the kinds of questions I asked, with some tentative results.

There would seem to be five basic prerequisites for a successful Russian reform: (1) a strong reformist leader, (2) a consolidated reformist constituency, (3) an adequate strategy of reform, (4) a favorable international environment—or at least the absence of an adverse environment, and (5) a proper sequence of reformist steps. Of the ten major Russian reform attempts I analyzed there was not one instance in which all of the prerequisites were present. The third prerequisite, for example, was lacking in all ten cases. What is of most immediate interest, however, is that in three of the ten cases (two in the twentieth century) the major cause of failure was the adverse international environment. One of these was the reform attempt of the 1960s.

*   *   *

Of the ten reformist cases, I was able to analyze only four in detail—those of the 1550s, the 1600s, the 1720s, and the 1960s. An attempt to rely on the work of other scholars for the rest proved unsatisfactory: too much depends on one's angle of vision. It is clear that it might take many more years to complete the endeavor. However, if I read the present Soviet domestic situation accurately, it seems we may have little time to spare before the movement toward a new counterreform gets out of control—i.e., builds a momentum that would be extremely difficult if not impossible to stop. And if I read the present international situation correctly, the environment for a successful reform becomes more and more adverse. There can hardly be any doubt that, however paradoxical it may sound, the major beneficiaries of the present U.S. administration's endeavor to "rearm America" are the Soviet military, who are gaining much more from it in political terms than their American counterparts are gaining in military terms. Thus both the domestic and international environments appear to be pushing the Russian empire in the direction of a counterreform.

Faced with this frightening prospect, I decided to take the painful step of publishing this excerpt from my work in the hope of attracting public attention to the enormously complex and dangerous task faced by the reformist component of the Russian political equilibrium in the 1980s—that is, by the reformist Russia to which I once had the honor to belong. There is a chance, however slight, that I can help my Russia to find the sympathy and support in the West it so badly needs.

This, however, is not the only reason I decided that the publication of this case study is urgent.

*   *   *   *

This is the story of a remarkable phenomenon: a spectacular rise of the Russian peasantry from the ashes of its second serfdom. It is about a genuinely spontaneous and massive popular movement that swept like a forest fire through the Soviet villages in the 1960s. Once again, as in the 1920s, it split the peasants into two camps—a proud and industrious peasant elite and the "swamp"; once again it made manifest that the dynamic reformist potential of the Russian peasantry is still there after the Soviet serfdom as it was after the tsarist serfdom.

Peasant reforms have constituted the core or the supporting background of virtually every major reformist attempt in Russia since the mid-sixteenth century. The genuinely spontaneous character of this movement of the Russian peasantry in the 1960s challenges practically all the prevailing sovietological assumptions about the workings of Soviet society. The goals of the movement were quite realistic, and in fact were achieved in one of the provinces of the Soviet empire, although not in the imperial center, where the movement was brutally suppressed by the regime of political stagnation.[3] For this reason the analysis of the causes of its failure reveals much about the nature of Russian reform. But this does not fully explain why I deem the publication of this case study so urgent.

There are strong signs of some stirrings toward a new agricultural reform in post-Brezhnev Russia, which may portend a general reform attempt.[4] A very distressing aspect of what one reads nowadays in the Soviet press on this subject is a clear indication that, in terms of intellectual development, the new reformist stirrings of the 1980s are far behind where we were at the end of the 1960s—after a decade of

---

[3]In a way one might say that the Hungarians have adopted some of its major ideas, implementing what we dreamed of. In fact, many think that it is this agricultural reform that is the backbone of the spectacular Hungarian economic breakthrough of the 1970s. This also challenges the prevailing sovietological wisdom: the failure of the reform could not have been due simply to the communist character of the contemporary Russian/Soviet empire because Hungary is also a communist state.

[4]See, for example, *Sel'skaya zhizn'*, 3/23/83; *Economicheskaia gazeta*, No. 14, 1983; *Izvestia*, 4/1/83; *Pravda*, 4/14/83.

reformist experience. Our old and (as is now clear) fatal errors are being repeated, as if we hadn't paid for them dearly enough. Like the Bourbons, the Soviet leaders seem to learn nothing, but unlike the Bourbons, they forgot everything. No lessons seem to have been drawn from our defeat by those who are now writing on the subject.

I had known the people involved in making the reform of the 1960s—the rural managers, the peasant elite of the Soviet villages, the journalists, the academics. I had worked with them; I was one of them. I also knew those who had opposed and ultimately crushed the reform—the party professionals, the village officials, the orthodox scholars, the "priests" of Soviet agriculture. I had fought them in private and public debates. In fact I had devoted a good part of the "best and brightest" years of my life to the reform.

My old comrades-in-arms are by now either dead—or scared to death and silenced. Someone has to tell the people involved in the new movement how dangerous the path is they are now setting out on, how subtle and complex the difficulties are, how much intellectual sophistication they will require, and how dearly they will pay for defeat—with disgrace, exile, or even death. I know this because my generation of Russian reformers already paid this terrible price in the 1970s. My memories may be needed by the new generation.

*   *   *   *   *

Along with Ivan Khudenko, to whose memory this work is dedicated, Nikita Khrushchev is the hero of my book. Khrushchev was without doubt one of the most controversial figures in Russian political history (perhaps only Dimitrii the Impostor of 1605 is comparable to him in this respect). The builder of the Berlin Wall and the instigator of the Cuban Missile Crisis, the man who once made the unfortunate mistranslated and misinterpreted boast "We will bury you" to an audience of Westerners,[5] Khrushchev is the embodiment of evil in the eyes of many. For others he was a reckless and erratic "voluntarist" associated with failed "harebrained

---

[5]The literal translation is "We will outlive you." The closest equivalent in colloquial English is perhaps "We will dance on your grave." It should by no means be interpreted as anything like "We intend to kill you," which unfortunately is how it is conventionally understood.

schemes," and for this reason a highly questionable reformer.[6] For still others Khrushchev was an "embattled consumer advocate" who, in George Breslauer's words, "led a pro-consumer faction within the Presidium against usually successful obstructionism by representatives of heavy industry and defense."

To be sure, it would have been much more desirable to see a Thomas Jefferson at the helm of post-Stalin Russia rather than a Nikita Khrushchev. Unfortunately, the choice was not between Khrushchev and someone like Jefferson but between Khrushchev and someone like Molotov, who almost certainly would never have saved, let alone rehabilitated, millions of innocent victims perishing in the Stalinist Gulag. It was Khrushchev who saved them, and if he had done nothing else, he would deserve our admiration. But he did much more. As I will try to show in this book, Nikita Khrushchev did more to prevent a new Russian counterreform than any other leader in the twentieth century after Stolypin and Bukharin were violently removed from the Russian political scene. No doubt he had his limitations—Khrushchev's life is full of human and political errors, of poor judgments and ill-timed eruptions. And yet it was he—not Malenkov, not Molotov, not Bulganin, nor any other graduate of the Stalinist academy of terror—who found the inner strength to challenge the very foundations of the monstrous system under the spell of which he had grown up, to attack his former allies who brought him to power, to boldly attempt to change what seemed unchangeable. It is this Khrushchev—the reformer—for whom I stand unflinchingly, fully realizing the relative validity of my judgment. In this I join Sir Isaiah Berlin, who ended his lecture "Two Concepts of Liberty" with a superb quotation from an unnamed source: "To realize the relative validity of one's convictions and yet stand for them unflinchingly is what distinguishes a civilized man from a barbarian."[7]

---

[6]This is the official view in post-Khrushchev Russia. The most prominent exponent of this view in American sovietology is Jerry Hough. A recent book by George Breslauer also lends itself to such an interpretation (*Khrushchev and Brezhnev as Leaders* [London: Allen and Unwin, 1982]).

[7]Isaiah Berlin, *Russian Thinkers* (Penguin Books, 1978), p. xxiii.

*　　*　　*　　*　　*　　*

There is one more thing I wish to add for the readers of this "prologue" to the drama of the Soviet peasantry. Those who feel uncomfortable, confused, or simply curious at encountering in this book some terms which sound strange in a Soviet context (terms like "parliamentary caucus," "post-totalitarian state," "Soviet Protestantism," or "metropolitan elites") will find an explanation of what I mean by them in *Notes on Terminology* at the end of the text. These theoretical terms are basic to my overall conceptual framework, and an understanding of them is essential to a full comprehension of my views on the role of reform in general and of the Link Reform of the 1960s in particular in the Russian/Soviet polity.

Chapter 1

THE SYSTEM

SHOP-WINDOW SHOCK

The first thing Soviet emigrés experience on coming to the West (usually to Vienna) is an astonishing psychological disturbance which someone has called "shop-window shock." As if hypnotized, they wander through the streets for hours, looking at the incredible variety and abundance of things exhibited in the shop-windows (most notably things to eat), not believing their eyes. A Lucullan feast, a bacchanalia of temptation, a satanic triumph of gastronomy! The Viennese residents do not notice this display—or to be more precise, they take it as a matter of course. Eventually the emigrés themselves cease to notice it, but during those first days they're dumbfounded.

They have come from a world which has declared itself to be the highest achievement of mankind, the embodiment of good on earth and the triumph of reason—but a world of incredible scarcity which they were used to, just as the Viennese are used to the abundance of their world, because it is part of their everyday existence. They have come from empty shop shelves, from exhausting queues, from chronic food crisis which has compelled them to spend half their lives on elementary survival. And they have come into a world which acknowledges its defects, but in which people do not merely survive but thrive. An invisible barrier separates the two worlds: one proclaims itself to be the future of mankind but proves in fact to be the past—a dark, medieval prison of the soul and the flesh—while in the other a renaissance market of ideas competes in abundance with the market of goods.

Above all, perhaps, "shop-window shock" is experienced by the emigré as an indictment of Soviet "collective" agriculture—as indisputable proof of its failure. The remedy seems obvious. If the plenty of the West has been created by independent farmers and the Soviet

1

THE SYSTEM

scarcity by "collective" agriculture, isn't the natural solution to replace the latter with independent farmers? This is what the Russian
emigrés usually propose.[1] But how is it to be done? By persuading
the Communist leadership to renounce Communist ideology?[2] By
inciting mass revolution?[3] By engineering a military coup?[4] Any of
these remains far beyond the capabilities of the poor emigrés, who
have no power either to bring about these changes or to control what
happened if they were to occur. This is all in the realm of utopian
dreams, which have always been the privilege of exiles. These dreams
are seductive, but they are incapable of affecting the real state of
affairs—either the stagnation of Soviet agriculture or the chronic food
crisis of which it is the primary cause.

Reformist Russia in the 1960s did not enjoy this emigré privilege. It was not attracted by seductive dreams—however tempting—
because it had things to do. It sought to propose a concrete, practical
plan which would perhaps, in the final analysis, bring about a revolution in the Soviet countryside, but which would look like a constructive alternative, not challenging the regime's ideological principles,
and therefore able to mobilize powerful interest groups within the
establishment. The question was whether such an intermediate scheme

[1] A return to private farming is perhaps the only point on which emigré publi-
cations of all tendencies agree—from *Posev* [Sowing], striving for anti-Communist revolution, to *Russkoe vozrozhdenie* [The Russian renaissance], striving for
the restoration of monarchy, to *Kontinent*, which vacillates from right to left
and back again, to the imperial monarchist *Golos zarubezh'ia* [The voice from
abroad]. This solution is also popular in the West. See, for example, *Newsweek*:
"[Since] the private plots now permitted on the fringes of the huge collective
farms [which] make up only 3 percent of the nation's arable land . . . produce
about 30 percent of its food, . . . the solution for many of the Soviet Union's
agricultural problems seems simple: allow more private farming" (1/5/81, p. 25).
The sophisticated *Economist*, however, notes that "party leaders are unlikely
in the foreseeable future to contemplate de-collectivisation under any name"
(10/15/80, p. 21).

[2] See A. Solzhenitsyn, *Pis'mo vozhdiam Sovetskogo Souiza* [Letter to Soviet
leaders] (Paris: YMCA Press, 1974).

[3] See, for example, D. Panin, *Zapiski Sologdina* [Sologdin's notes] (Frankfurt-
am-Main, 1973). See also I. Matskevich, "S nekotorym otkloneniem ot temy"
[A little off the point], *Golos zarubezh'ia* 18 (1980): 5-9.

[4] See A. Solzhenitsyn, interview with the BBC, February 1979; printed in
Vestnik RkhD 127 (1979): 272, 294-95.

2

could be found—between the dream of those who sought the destruction of collective agriculture and the stubborn determination of powerful party "priests" to preserve the Stalinist heritage—to freeze the Soviet countryside in kolkhozy and sovkhozy.[5] At first glance this might seem an impossible challenge. The primary purpose of this section is to show how such a scheme was found—and then rejected.

A decade of dramatic efforts was needed, a decade in which the labor, the intelligence and imagination, the talent, and the energy of thousands of people from all levels of society were engaged in working out this alternative and demonstrating its viability. In this effort, reformist Russia went significantly further than anything proposed by the liberal intelligentsia of Prague or Warsaw. The results were astounding, but, as we now know, they did not lead anywhere. "Link reform" of the Soviet countryside (as this alternative was called) did not come to fruition—just as the cultural renaissance of the 1960s did not take place. It was rejected at the same time that the *Novyi mir* party was routed and the two-party structure of the literary establishment eliminated. The most prominent leader of the Link reform, Ivan Khudenko, was convicted along with his collaborators, Mikhail Li and Viacheslav Filatov, on a false charge, and died in prison in 1974.

Were the efforts expended in working out this alternative wasted? It is not for me to judge, because I cannot be objective. As a participant in the reform, I travelled through well over half of the country—from the Amur province on the Chinese border to Kabardino-Balkaria in the Caucasus, and from Smolensk in the west to Tashkent in the south. I discussed it in dozens of articles and essays in magazines and newspapers. In many symposia and conferences devoted to this reform, I proselytized, entreated, argued, intrigued, and challenged authority. I did everything in my power to ensure the success of the reform and then to save it from ruin. I am among the losers. I am filled with grief and despair, so what kind of a judge can I be? It

---

[5]There were in the 1960s 29,000 *kolkhozy* (collective farms) and 18,000 *sovkhozy* (state farms) in the USSR. Between the kolkhozy and the sovkhozy there are a number of differences, but from the point of view of organization and payment for labor, with which we are chiefly concerned here, these differences are insignificant. For the sake of brevity, we will henceforth refer to the form of collective agriculture which exists in the USSR as the kolkhoz system.

is better that the reader judge for himself the results of our struggle. My task is to relate with the maximum possible objectivity what I have witnessed. I am not equipped to write a history of the Link Reform. I will tell only what I have seen, felt, and thought, and what conclusions I have drawn from my experiences. I will tell about a revolution which never came—one result of which was, in the following decade, the "shop-window shock" of the Soviet emigrés.

HISTORY STOPPED

The peasant community in Europe is essentially a remnant of the preindustrial age. From the time of the Industrial Revolution, European history has been made in the cities. Production requiring highly developed skills, science, administration, commerce, and art— all of these have been concentrated in cities. The peasant community became only a source of raw materials—in the form of goods and people. It fed the cities not only with grain and milk but also with healthy and talented youth. This led to the exhaustion of the human resources of the countryside and, in the final analysis, to the end of the peasant community, which has largely been replaced by scattered, highly industrialized farms with a minimum population living on the land, but still able to supply the cities with the food products they need. Not everywhere in Europe has it gone this far, but such is apparently the inevitable direction of development: the more highly industrialized the agriculture, the more the peasant community is replaced by individual farmers.

In Russia this natural development was arrested by Stalin's collectivization drive. First, the most energetic and enterprising part of the peasantry, its elite, which was capable of forming the nucleus of a body of individual farmers, was "de-kulakized"—that is, robbed and exiled to the distant northern regions. Everyone who tried to resist was swallowed up by Stalin's Gulag. Millions of people were involved, and the Russian countryside was deprived of the human material necessary for its natural development.

Second, after collectivization the countryside was transformed into an object of military-feudal exploitation by the state. It was crushed with taxes, and everything which it produced was taken from it. It was not even left enough grain to feed itself. In the kolkhozy,

4

people essentially worked for nothing, deprived of any incentive whatever. They survived only thanks to their tiny household plots on which they grew potatoes—the bread of the Russian poor.

Here lay the somber mastery of Stalin's agrarian plan, which was able to avert both the development of a powerful corps of individual farmers, on the one hand, and the proletarianization of the countryside recommended by Marxist doctrinaires—that is, the transformation of the peasants into agricultural workers—on the other. In the latter case, the peasants would have had to be paid. Under Stalin's ingenious plan, they provided their own food and worked for the state like serfs. The result was a quarter-century triumph of state serfdom. History stopped for the Russian countryside: it was preserved in its medieval form.

The price paid for this was horrendous. Even now, after the advent of the post-totalitarian era apparently has changed everything in the countryside—when tractors and other heavy-duty machines are streaming into the farms, when the peasants are paid for their labor and their private plots are no longer overburdened with taxes but, on the contrary, encouraged by the state, and when country people have finally obtained internal passports enabling them to leave the villages[6]—even now the countryside remains both a heavy fetter on the legs of the Soviet economy and an open wound in Soviet society. Its situation is essentially the same as it was a century ago after the abolition of serfdom—but in contrast to then, it is unable to feed the cities.

All of this is more or less common knowledge, but I am including a short historical account here in order to explain why the de-Stalinization of the countryside seemed so important to the reformist Russia of the 1960s, why the Link Reform was the centerpiece of its program, and why it was able to recruit to its cause defenders from all

---

[6]Until 1981, peasants who did not have the internal passports required for registering in the city were bound to the land, and their movements were strictly regulated by the state. This did not prevent them from migrating to the cities on their own, but such migration was illegal. The channels of peasant migration are considered in detail in my essay "Trevogi Smolenshchiny. Sotsiologicheskii ocherk," part 1, *Literaturnaia gazeta*, 7/27/66. For English translation, see "The Tribulations of the Smolensk Countryside," *International Journal of Sociology* 6, 2-3 (Summer-Fall 1976) [hereafter *IJS*], pp. 24-33.

walks of life—including me, a city-dweller to the marrow of my bones, who in childhood believed that bagels grew on trees.[7]

COLLECTIVE FARM SOCIETY

Let us look first at how the Soviet countryside—in its predominant kolkhoz form—is constructed, what groups it consists of, how it is administered, and why it doesn't work.

In formal terms, the kolkhoz is a classic case of direct democracy—a kind of joint stock company or, more accurately, a free self-governing commune, which is called upon once a year to decide its fate at a general assembly by electing a governing board. The term *kolkhoz democracy* was as popular in the 1960s as the term *socialist democracy*. (The temptation to see in the former a kind of miniature model of the latter has proved irresistible.)

In the summer of 1966 I visited dozens of general assemblies in the kolkhozy of Tambov province (in central Russia). This was a risky and in some ways unique experiment both in a journalistic sense and as an analysis of kolkhoz democracy, which up to that time had never been described, with the result that the Soviet people had no better understanding of it than people in the West. To my surprise—and, it must be added, to the surprise of the editors of *Komsomol'skaia pravda* who had sent me to Tambov—my essay "The Kolkhoz Assembly" was approved for publication. Some passages were deleted by the editors and others by the censors, but the essential nucleus remained intact. The substance of the essay is reproduced here, with the deleted material restored from memory.

---

[7] At first, in the early 1960s, my adventures as a correspondent for Moscow newspapers and journals in rural districts were reminiscent of Mark Twain's story "How I Edited a Farmer's Paper." Once, for example, while tramping across the fields with the Minister of Irrigation of the Kabardin Republic, I commented on the luxuriant growth of weeds along our path. "That is hemp, young man, not weeds," the Minister responded devastatingly. Much water has flowed under the bridge since then. I studied diligently, not only poring over thick textbooks on agriculture but also spending days on end in the fields with tractor drivers, and only a year after the Minister's annihilating reply, chairmen of kolkhozy were discussing their problems with me quite seriously.

So then, here is a kolkhoz assembly. A few hundred people are gathered in a village clubhouse on a Sunday. They sit there, surrounded by clouds of tobacco smoke, facing the fly-spotted portraits of party leaders, seven or eight hours at a stretch, fiercely cracking sunflower seeds with their teeth, squabbling with one another and deciding their fate. In this sense, the meeting is reminiscent of a play put on by a single director in many theaters on the basis of the same script. The back rows (the "gallery") are occupied by people who have had time to "wet their whistles" before the work of the meeting begins. The chairmen of the kolkhozy and the presidium of the assemblies occupying the stage refer to these people as "loudmouths." Throughout the meeting they severely repress the quite unparliamentary expressions emanating almost without interruption from the gallery, accompanied by passionate demands for "the floor." However, the gallery is not given the floor. On the contrary, when the swearing becomes unbearable, the loudmouths are led from the hall on the arms of specially appointed strongmen. As far as can be understood from the gallery's rather indistinct shouts, their critique is not constructive in a political or economic sense. It is, rather, personal and denunciatory in character. From it, one can find out certain details which are in a sense shocking, but not the most essential for the functioning of the kolkhoz. It relates chiefly to such topics as the private life of the chairman or the quantity of liquor consumed by the honored presidium in the time left free from its honorary tasks. By listening more attentively, one might learn of the suspicious source of additional income of the accountant, or about the agronomist's ungentlemanly treatment of his wife. All in all, it can be concluded that these people are in principle opposed to management—chiefly local management. Their turn of mind when tipsy is rather anarchistic.

On the front benches sit those in the upper reaches of kolkhoz society—those who have some connection with management (from the party organizer to the bookkeeper), people with specialized occupations (tractor drivers and milkmaids), and also the old men of the generation which remembers the times before collectivization. They are very active and talkative, these old men; they make long, fiery speeches, the gist of which is that the young people of today do not *want* to do, do not *know how* to do, and *will* not do the work of peasants. In this torrent of eloquence, penetrating notes of bitterness sometimes sound which astound even the chairmen. The old men are

7

confused. After half a century of life in kolkhozy, they still do not understand their status as "collective owners of the land." Consider, they say, a particular field. One person plows it, another throws seed on it, a third cultivates it, and a fourth harvests from it a crop which he has not sown—and each one thinks only of his wages. Who is concerned for Mother Earth herself—for what *she* needs in order to feed us? Who thinks of her at all? There are no such people in the kolkhoz, which means there are no owners, only consumers. The land is perishing as an orphan. The old men prophesy a terrible, starved future. However, they do not propose anything concrete to correct the situation. Their criticism is more apocalyptical and philosophical than anything else; it is bitter and profound but abstract.

The tractor drivers and milkmaids, on the other hand, criticize so narrowly and specifically that their criticism lacks practical value. They scold the brigadiers for not fertilizing the fields, pronounce anathemas on the drivers for not bringing water on time, denounce the chairman for not hunting up towels for the milkmaids, and so on for hours on end. The kolkhozniks with skilled occupations make up about third of all the "stockholders," but even they are not capable of articulating group interests or the interests of the collective farm as a whole.

The center of the hall is dominated by the "swamp"—a stable majority, solid as a monolith, which views with delight the struggle between the presidium and the gallery, cracks sunflower seeds, laughs at the old men, and takes an interest in the meeting only as a spectacle. It does not participate in the debate and in general acts more like the orchestra audience in a theater than like a group of stockholders.

The show has three acts. The first act is devoted to the chairman's reports and the report of the inspection committee. During the intermission, questions are asked—and this is the real beginning of the drama. In the second act, the debates take place, and here differences of opinion become sharpest and passions are hottest, only to die down suddenly in the third and final act—the election of the governing board. The people are tired, and do not hide the fact that they are bored. There are no election committees and no one counts the votes. At the meeting at the Red Communard kolkhoz, the chairman didn't even ask for the aye vote.

The average chairman's report, by my calculations, contains about one thousand figures. The report of the inspection committee contains somewhat less. While the chairman, in order to hold the attention of the audience, includes a variety of interesting anecdotes, the report of the inspection committee is pure statistics—a kind of orgy of statistics. It took me as much as two weeks to decipher one of these reports. It is inconceivable that the "stockholders" could at once digest such a report, make comparisons, and determine whether they had gotten richer or gone bankrupt in the past year. Chairmen do not like kolkhoz assemblies, and describe them as "occasions for shouting and demagogy." Their reports are full of self-criticism and sometimes even self-flagellation (the chairman of the Red Communard kolkhoz described some of his actions as "reckless"), but because they lack any analysis of the underlying economic processes, the picture they present—despite the self-flagellation—tends to be reassuring.

Neither in the reports nor in the debates does anyone touch upon the fundamental truth that the grain harvest in all of these kolkhozy has remained for many years at a shamefully low level for the Black Earth region (11-12 tsentners per hectare) and shows no tendency to increase. This land *can* yield (and in some cases which will be discussed below) *does* yield 60-70 tsentners per hectare. In other words, the kolkhozy of Tambov province realize only 15-20 percent of the productive potential of their land. The harvest of millet is 6 tsentners per hectare, and of sugar beets 28 tsentners. Any kolkhoznik obtains an equal amount from the five-hundredths of a hectare of his own garden plot.

If we dig a little deeper, we find more. For example, it turns out that the production yield per ruble of funds invested in the Red Communard kolkhoz declined over the course of five years from 126 kopecks to 97. In effect, the kolkhoz is going bankrupt. As its invested funds—that is, the value of its farm buildings and equipment—increase, the efficiency of their use falls. This is even more evident in the Lenin's Spark kolkhoz, where the invested funds increased over a five-year period by 110,000 rubles while the value of production increased by only 17,000. It turns out that money is being spent without results. Increasing the complexity of the operation leads to its decline. The kolkhoz seems to be a bottomless pit.

We have spoken of the "upper reaches" and the "swamp" of the kolkhoz. If we look into its account books, the origin of this distinction becomes clear. Soviet statistics prefer to speak of the income of the "collective farm peasantry," leaving us in ignorance of the different incomes of its various groups. In this generalized form, the income figures look fairly decent. In the 1960s, when the average wage in the USSR (approximately equal to the minimum necessary for survival) was around 120 rubles per month, the "collective farm peasantry" earned 90 rubles. But this figure conceals a very essential point without which we cannot understand the mechanics of kolkhoz life. While the chairman of the kolkhoz received 300 rubles per month, the agronomists 170, the brigadiers 120, and the milkmaids and tractor drivers 90, all the others—the so-called "horse-and-hand workers"—received no more than 30 rubles per month. In other words, two-thirds of rural society earns no more than 25 percent of the minimum necessary for survival from work on the kolkhoz. Their material well-being does not depend on the success or failure of the kolkhoz; they are on their own. By far the larger share of their earnings derives from the sale of meat, milk, or potatoes grown on their private plots. This is the explanation for the merry indifference of those in the orchestra seats to the questions considered at the kolkhoz assemblies: what happens in the kolkhoz will not make them any richer or poorer.

Here we are confronted with the astonishing fact that the greater part of the immense rural population of the USSR—many times larger than the farm population of the United States—has only a marginal interest in the collective economy and takes only a marginal part in it. In practical terms, this means that the kolkhoz system is in a position to use the productive potential of only 30-35 percent of the manpower resources of the Soviet countryside. The other 65-70 percent of the peasants work in the kolkhoz only the minimum number of hours necessary to prevent their being deprived of the right to use their household plots—and that is the extent of their relations with the kolkhoz.

It may seem that positions have been reversed—that the elite is concentrated in the orchestra of the kolkhoz assembly hall, since the incomes of its members are determined by their own labor and initiative, and their degree of independence from management is incomparably greater than that of the people with specialized occupations—but this is a misleading impression. It can arise only in the mind of a city-dweller who has a specialized occupation, an apartment with all the conveniences, an eight-hour-or-so working day, an established salary and days off, and who does not have any animals to feed, except perhaps a dog or cat. The kolkhoz orchestra has an Achilles' heel: its way of life is completely dependent on the will of one person. Here the similarity of the kolkhoz to a stock company or to an ordinary business enterprise ends, and cruel reality begins. In the kolkhoz, people not only earn their incomes together and work together, but they also live together. If you are a member of a stock company and the ceiling in your house begins to leak, or there is no milk at the local store, or you get sick and have to go to the doctor, or you need fuel in the winter and building materials in the summer, or you need transport to take potatoes to market, you will hardly turn for help to the president of the company. You have many other ways to turn. The kolkhoznik has only one: all his roads lead to Rome—to the kolkhoz chairman. The chairman is the all-mighty who controls the distribution of fuel and building materials, allots fodder for the livestock and arranges transportation to deliver it, evaluates each member's work, grants permission to go to work or to stay home on Sunday, determines how many hours will be worked—and everything else. The chairman is both the manager of the kolkhoz and the leader of the rural community—the undisputed leader. Formally his powers are limited. According to the charter of the kolkhoz, he is only the "chairman of the governing board," and all his decisions must be approved by a majority of the board. Thus the governing board is expected to perform both the functions of administrators and of representatives of the community to limit the personal power of the leader by monitoring his activities. But can the governing board really perform this second monitoring function on which the well-being of the majority of collective farmers depends?

In the Lenin's Spark kolkhoz in 1965, the governing board included the chairman, two brigadiers, a deputy chairman, a mechanic, a warehouse supervisor, and a poultry specialist. In 1966, it included the chairman, three brigadiers, the deputy chairman, an agronomist, and the warehouse supervisor—that is, another brigadier in place of the mechanic, and an agronomist in place of the poultry specialist. As we can see, in 1965, only two of the seven members of the governing board—the mechanic and (to a degree) the poultry specialist—were people with specialized occupations, whose status and income did not depend on the will of the chairman. In 1966 there was only one independent specialist—the agronomist. All the others were "people without education or specialty (to quote from my essay

11

"The Kostroma Experiment") who can in practical terms be removed from their posts and tomorrow become 'horse-and-hand' kolkhozniks, which would mean, among other things, a several-fold decrease in their earnings."[8] Thus the institution which, according to the charter, is supposed to act as a control over the leader does not in fact—by virtue of its members' dependent status—exercise such control. "It is therefore not surprising (I observed in another essay) that the organ of collective leadership becomes . . . the expression of the will of one person."[9] In other words, the chairman is the autocrat of the kolkhoz society.

Bearing in mind that kolkhoz democracy was perceived as a microcosm of socialist democracy, this conclusion had devastating wider implications: the mechanism of "collective leadership"—both of the kolkhoz and of the state—had no guarantee against being transformed into an autocracy. My conclusion directly challenged the official concept of socialist democracy as the highest form of democracy in the world. This dissent from official doctrine was noteworthy, but what is considerably more important is that one of the most authoritative Soviet newspapers, after some hesitation, published it. I ended my report with the observation "A democracy which does not work [*read*: politically] will not work economically either: what other conclusion can follow?"[10]

Now let me add what a Soviet journalist cannot publish under any circumstances, but is understood by every one of his Soviet readers. It is no surprise that kolkhoz democracy does not work. That is what was intended. In the eyes of the boss standing directly above the autocrat of the kolkhoz—that is, the little Stalin on a district scale (the first secretary of the district committee of the party)—the chairman of the kolkhoz was the same as the brigadier in the chairman's eyes. He could be discharged by a single stroke of the boss's pen. He was not supposed to have roots in the community, or a constituency standing behind him. He was an official appointed and discharged at

[8]"Kostromskoi eksperiment. Sotsiologicheskii ocherk," *Literaturnaia gazeta*, 12/27/67. For English translation, see "The Kostroma Experiment," *IJS*, pp. 42-53.

[9]"Kolkhoznoe sobranie. Sotsiologicheskii ocherk," "*Komsomol'skaia pravda*, 7/5/66. For English translation, see "A Collective Farm Meeting," *IJS*, pp. 13-23.

[10]*Ibid*.

the discretion of the district autocrat—just as the latter could be discharged at the discretion of the provincial autocrat above him (the first secretary of the provincial committee of the party), and he in turn could at any moment be destroyed by the supreme autocrat. Such was the merciless Stalinist hierarchical "vertical principle"—from the bottom to the top, from the kolkhoz brigadier to the generalissimo who ruled over the country. It was a kind of occupation regime which sought to present itself to the world wrapped in a democratic toga.

In this way, a seemingly innocent analysis of a kolkhoz assembly became, for the sophisticated reader, a revelation of the true character of the state structure under which he was destined to live out his life. An investigation of the economic unworkability of kolkhoz democracy proved to be an explanation of the failure of socialist democracy in general. True, a Soviet journalist could not say this publicly even in the 1960s. On the other hand, he could at that time—unlike in preceding and subsequent decades—not only give his reader to understand that socialist democracy does not work, but also suggest alternatives to this non-working system—at least at the level of its microcosmic model in the kolkhoz. What I had in mind was the Link Reform, which—as we imagined in those times which now appear almost fabulous—seemed capable of serving as the starting point for a reform of the whole system.

A radical reform of the Soviet countryside, however, cannot be based on the old men, with their touchingly childlike openness, or on the politically indifferent horse-and-hand workers, interested only in the productivity of their household plots. The only ones who can become the nucleus and the soul of such a reform are educated, active, energetic young people, but the situation in the Soviet countryside for the young is bad.

DOES THE KOLKHOZ NEED EDUCATED YOUTH?

I had occasion to write several essays on this topic, which were among the bitterest of all those I wrote in Russia. Let us take as an example the Smolensk province, situated in the heartland of the country, in its long-suffering non-Black-Earth area. In 1965 the grain harvest there was 8.6 tsentners per hectare—the highest level in the past quarter century; the average yield was only 6 tsentners. In northern Germany or in the Netherlands the same kind of land yields the equivalent of 30 tsentners. Furthermore, in the 1960s there were yields on similar lands in the Moscow region, within the zone of the Link Reform, as high as 60 tsentners in individual cases, which demonstrated the true productive potential of these lands. In other words, the kolkhozy of the Smolensk area, like those of the Tambov region, produced only 10-20 percent of their potential output.

In Smolensk, however, the situation was even worse than in Tambov because, due to a mass exodus of the young, the kolkhozy did not have the prospect of maintaining even this limited production level. The changes in numbers of the Komsomol give us a notion of the pace of this exodus. (All children in the upper grades of schools belong to the Komsomol.) In 1960 there were 21,043 Komsomol members; in 1965 only 3,788 remained. In the village of Pomogailovo, the brigadier recalled that the last wedding was celebrated five years ago. There are villages where, as M. Kalmyk, first secretary of the Smolensk provincial committee told me, a child's voice has not been heard for years. In 1965, 4.5 times fewer children were born in the province than in 1940, and the natural increase of its rural population had been reduced by 17 times over the previous 17 years.[11] The villages in the Smolensk province are apparently dying away.

I conducted a survey of the older school children concerning their plans for the future, with these results: 65 percent of the eighth-graders, 83 percent of the tenth-graders, and 96 percent of the eleventh-graders were planning to leave the countryside. In other words, the higher the level of education, the higher the percentage planning to leave. Why?

In the Soviet press, this exodus from the countryside is usually explained by the shortage of rural clubhouses, the lack of entertainment and cultural facilities and the other things the city can provide, and the desire to escape from the 10-12 hour working day. However, the situation is more complex than this: the kolkhoz system has no place for the educated young. Just as it is not able to exploit the productive potential of the land or the human resources of the countryside, so it cannot make use of the education or the skills of the youth—cannot offer them social mobility, or an adequate income, or

[11]A. Yanov, "Trevogi Smolenshchiny," pp. 24-33.

an arena for applying their expertise. It is not surprising that almost 90 percent of middle management of the kolkhozy have no more than primary education. This would seem to be highly improbable in a province where during the seven years from 1958 to 1965, 4,973 persons with higher or specialized secondary education were sent to work in kolkhozy—enough to fill more than a half of all the managerial positions. However, it is what you will find in every kolkhoz, in every province. Let us take as an example the Andreevskii kolkhoz in Kostroma province in northern Russia:

> [Here] there are 12 brigadiers. How many of them are young? None. Are there among them people who have even 8 years of education? Not one. Look at the makeup of the managing board of the kolkhoz. Both in 1964 and in 1966, of the thirteen members of the board, 10 had only primary education, and only two were under 30. Educated young people take almost no part in administration. There are no avenues for the application of their intellectual and creative potential.[12]

But why does this happen? I did not find the answer to this question in the impoverished Russian northwest. I found it in Belgorod province, in the Black Earth zone of southern Russia, in the relatively successful experimental Frunze kolkhoz.

AN AUTOCRAT IN SPITE OF HIMSELF

Vasilii Gorin, chairman of the kolkhoz, is a gifted and educated person, a brilliant organizer, one of those "new managers" who are sick to death of distributing fuel, fodder, and building materials to the kolkhozniks. He is a man with ideas; he does not want to be an autocrat. He is attracted not by power, but by action, by the opportunity to apply his ideas. He is tormented and humiliated by the impoverished condition of the Soviet countryside. His dream is to see it rich and competitive. In the summer of 1969, I found him alarmed and upset: matters were not going well. And the most distressing thing was that he could not make out at all why they were not going well. Here is an example of what was tormenting him.

[12]"Kostromskoi eksperiment."

He conducted a pre-harvest meeting in one of the brigades. For him this was an exalted and solemn moment. He spoke beautifully, putting his soul into his speech, like a general on the eve of a decisive battle. That for which they had prepared for a whole year and on which an immense amount of effort, money, skill, and devotion had been expended would be realized the next day in a brief, intense effort of will. The outcome of the battle depended on each warrior in particular, and on all of them jointly. But Gorin's warriors showed no sign of sharing their general's exaltation. They remained as indifferent to it as the "orchestra" at the meeting.[13] However, this time it was not the horse-and-hand workers whom the chairman addressed on the battlefield (so to speak), but the tractor drivers—that is, people from that segment of the participants in kolkhoz production from whom, it would seem, he could expect a positive response. But his expectations were shattered: the tractor drivers were no more interested in production than their horse-and-hand colleagues.

"Why aren't they interested in the common cause? We were told that you have to pay people well, and they will then work like blazes. So we do pay them well, but they don't work like blazes," said Gorin in desperation. "Why do they have to be constantly prompted, monitored, propagandized? Why do I, instead of developing management strategies, have to serve as a people-chaser and a fixer? Why do my young specialists have to work not like managers, but like officers of surveillance?"

It seemed indeed strange that in an experimental kolkhoz where one-fifth of all the specialists in the district were concentrated (there were 57 of them in the Frunze kolkhoz), there was not one educated person in middle management. Many times Gorin had tried to promote young managers with university educations to key posts, but the matter had always ended either with their leaving or with their having to be removed. They did not want and did not know how to serve as officers of surveillance. The problem was not only one of near total indifference to production on the part of the kolkhozniks under surveillance. What was worse was that all of their peasant shrewdness was directed toward fooling the management, putting one over on

[13]A. Yanov, "Pomogite sil'nomu. Sotsiologicheskii ocherk," *Molodoi kommunist*, No. 2, 1970, p. 57. For English translation, see "Help the Strong," *IJS*, pp. 64-74.

them, getting as much as possible for doing as little as possible. Under these conditions, the work of the junior managers had to be reduced chiefly to surveillance. Gorin knew that young managers would not tolerate this and would run away from it, and he would again be left with the uneducated and unskilled, and his dream would remain a dream. He knew it, but he could not help it.

Now we can see why educated youth run away from the kolkhoz: the two are simply incompatible. At the same time we are able to see why the kolkhoz in its present-day form is an autocracy: it cannot help but be one. Even under conditions where the autocrat himself does not want his dictatorship, and tries to end it, he remains its prisoner. This means that the fault does not lie in the evil will of the kolkhoz autocrat, or even in the Stalinist hierarchical vertical principle. The root of the problem of the kolkhoz autocracy must lie still deeper.

AN ARTEL' OF SHABASHNIKS

Before proceeding further I must explain certain terms which are not translatable into English, but are crucial for understanding kolkhoz life and, what is more important, the Link Reform. The *artel'* is a small traditional Russian peasant organization whose members work and are paid as a unit and divide the pay equally among themselves. A *shabashnik* is an independent contract worker, often migratory, who can be hired (individually or as part of a group) either by private individuals or by enterprises for specific jobs, usually of construction or repair. Companies of shabashniks, travelling on their own across the vast expanses of rural Russia, represented—before the appearance of the links—the only genuine form of the peasant artel' left from the old days.

It so happened that after his ill-fated speech on the "battlefield," Gorin and I had gone to a construction site. The people working there were hired builders come from the distant Caucasus—an artel' of shabashniks. How they worked! With what cheerful fervor, with what zeal and generosity! It did the heart good to look at them. Who was there to make fiery speeches at? On the contrary, the builders complained vehemently to the chairman: they had not been brought materials in time, and as a result they had stood idle for an hour! How must the chairman have felt listening to them when his kolkhozniks, unless they were constantly prompted, would twiddle their thumbs for days on end? With the kolkhozniks it was necessary day after day to make resolutions such as "[The brigadiers] must not allow their subordinates to be drunk during working hours.... The administration is compelled to demand accountability of the above-mentioned comrades for their inactivity in connection with drunkenness."[14]

Drunkenness during working hours is only the tip of the iceberg of kolkhoznik irresponsibility and indifference—only the symbol of them. One can demand accountability for drunkenness, and can try to eliminate it by rigorous administrative measures, but this will be only the elimination of a symbol—not of indifference itself. Administrative measures can perhaps eradicate an evil, but they cannot implant good—that is, stimulate the tractor drivers to work like the hired artel', joyfully, with pleasure. The chairman had not the slightest notion what kind of norms these people had, or how the work of each was evaluated. No one controlled these people because there was no need to control them.

"What the hell is this?," Gorin asked me. "Why do these people work when my kolkhozniks won't?"

"Pay attention to the quality of their work." (I rubbed some salt into his wounds.) "They work flawlessly, as kolkhoz tractor drivers never do. Do you check their work after it is finished?"

"There's no need of that," Gorin shrugged. "I know from experience that it's all fixed up to a T."

Why then was the quality of the work of the company of shabashniks so far superior to that of the work of the kolkhozniks? After all, they also were not individual farmers, but an artel'—i.e., a collective. But in contrast to the kolkhoz, theirs was a *working* collective. Gorin and I analyzed its structure, and this is what we discovered.

First, all the members are professionals and masters of their trade. (Incompetents or slackers are not accepted into the artel'.) Second, their payment is by contract for the final result of their work, whether this is a cow barn or a palace. No one calculates how

[14]A. Yanov, "V chem oshibaiutsia storonniki 'mozgovogo tresta.' Razmyshleniia o kolkhoznoi demokratii" [Where do the proponents of the "brain trust" make their mistake? Reflections on kolkhoz democracy], *Literaturnaia gazeta*, 6/4/69.

many stones each worker lays or how fast each of them mixes cement. All work for one goal, and each has confidence in everyone else. Third, the size of the artel' (9-11 persons) makes it very manageable, permitting the kind of internal monitoring which is impossible in a kolkhoz brigade made up of 200-300 people, where each one works by the piece—that is, according to established norms—concerned only for his wage, and where only the brigadier is answerable for the final result.

"But the wage of each tractor driver also depends on how the brigade as a whole works," Gorin protested.

"That's right," I said. But how can the individual tractor driver influence the results of the work of the brigade except by his personal labor? What is his guarantee that all the others will also work conscientiously and not be drunk during working hours? He cannot monitor his colleagues, so he turns the monitoring function over to the brigadier, who precisely in this way is changed into an overseer, a chaser. And that isn't the end of the matter. The brigadier cannot—no matter how hard he tries—keep track of several hundred people, spread over an immense space, some of whom plow the earth, while others load fertilizer, and still others carry water around. The brigadier needs assistants, bookkeepers, clerks, informers. As a result, an immense staff of overseers—on some kolkhozy it reaches 40 percent of all workers— gallops over the fields combing out slackers and violators. But even this isn't the whole thing. To discover those who are lying drunk under their tractors, or who have driven to the bazaar in their trucks during working hours, is relatively easy. But how is the depth of plowing to be measured for each tractor driver? How is one to check the speed at which he drives the tractor?

At that point I told him the following story.

THE SYSTEM OF MUTUAL MISTRUST

It happened on the Kuban' river in the Krasnodar region, in Soviet "Iowa," where the soil is infinitely rich. As they say: if you poke a stick into it, the stick will bloom. (Nevertheless, even in this area the average yield in the kolkhozy was never above 25 tsentners per hectare.) Here Aleksandr Erkaev, chief technologist of the Kuban' Institute for Testing of Agricultural Machinery—a serious, intelligent man and a good scientist—was struck by a phenomenon which seemed just as inexplicable to him as the success of the shabashnik artel' seems to you. He had developed new equipment for cultivating corn. It had worked well on an experimental field, and it seemed that he was on the verge of a breakthrough. But everything changed as if by magic as soon as he transferred his experiments to the kolkhoz field. There his equipment no longer performed properly. Why? When Erkaev investigated the matter, he discovered what had gone wrong. The equipment he had developed required precise handling: the shoots had to be harrowed at no greater speed than 2.5 km per hour. A tractor with a light harrow can do 24 km. As soon as the overseer turned away from the tractor driver (he couldn't follow him all day!), the driver put the tractor up to full speed—and immediately fulfilled the norm three, four, or five times over. Where he had done this, there was naturally no harvest.

On the other hand, you can understand the behavior of the tractor driver. For fulfilling the norm, he got 3 rubles; for three norms, 9 rubles; for five norms, 20 rubles. Now look what you get: the more the tractor driver earns, the less harvest there is. In other words, the incentives he is offered ensure that there will be no harvest.[15] Can you imagine that a peasant whose life depends on this harvest—or the shabashnik artel', which receives its wages for the final results of its labor—would ever act as the kolkhoz tractor driver acts every day and every hour? Such is the organic defect of the kolkhoz system of external controls, with its piecework and total surveillance. It inevitably counterposes the quantity of labor to its quality. More than that, it seems to reject innovation much as a body rejects a foreign organism. And no amount of surveillance can change this.

Here are some more examples. The peas are ripe in the field. Can you say what the harvest is going to be? No, you can't, because that depends on who will do the harvesting. The peasant artel' begins the harvest with the dew, at five in the morning, as peasants have done ever since there have been peasants. The kolkhozniks begin at 8 AM, when the peas have already dried out—and half of the crop is left in the fields. With soybeans, on the other hand, the situation is just the reverse. If the harvest is begun with the dew or early in the

[15]A. Yanov. "Spor s predsedatelem," *Literaturnaia gazeta*, 8/7/68. For English translation, see "A Dispute with the Chairman," *IJS*, pp. 54-63.

morning, you get very little. The peasant knows these things by heart, but the kolkhoz tractor driver has no reason to remember them because he cares nothing about them. His job is to fulfill his norm. And it can't be helped. It is not by accident that the kolkhoz system rejects not only technical innovation but also peasant common sense. It is not by accident that it destroys the peasant in the peasant, day by day, year in and year out. It was conceived this way and built accordingly. Its primary purpose was not production on the land, but total control over the peasant and the manager. For this you need mutual mistrust, mutual suspicion, and mutual surveillance—in brief, adversarial relations between the employer and the employees. It is in this negative, hostile environment that the peasant comes to hate the manager, as the actions of the "loudmouths" in the back rows show, and the manager to hate the peasant. In order to function, such a system must become an autocracy.

Looking retrospectively at this creation of Stalin's, we can see that for his purposes the kolkhoz system was constructed ideally. On one side, the managers were compelled to keep their eyes on the peasant every moment, while on the other, the peasants tried in every way to escape the control of the managers, to fool or embarrass them—thus ensuring that they would never relax their control. . . . This was my story—and such were the conclusions logically following from it.

In sum, the fundamental difference between the two collectives—the artel' and the kolkhoz—lies in their functions: the function of the artel' is economic; the function of the kolkhoz is political. One is oriented toward production; the other, toward control. This is why Vasilii Gorin is compelled to remain an autocrat against his will. He is not supposed to collaborate with the peasants: he is supposed to fight with them. If we remember for a moment the history of Russian rulers since the eighteenth century, all of whom have lived in constant fear of Pugachevism—the volcanic explosion of the elemental force of the peasantry which shook the whole Empire[16]—then we will not underestimate the terrible achievement of the great "peasant wrestler" (as the witty Osip Mandel'shtam called Stalin). There have been many tyrants in Russian history, but only the last of them broke the back

[16]The term *Pugachevism* derives from a peasant uprising led by Emel'ian Pugachev in 1773-74 which left the Russian aristocracy badly shaken.

of the peasantry. What the great tsarist peasant wrestler of the nine-teenth century, Arakcheev, who tried to force the peasants into military settlements, did not succeed in, Stalin was able to do. He created a kolkhoz autocracy which required total control by the chairman and the brigadiers over the peasantry, and this in turn was transformed into a system of total control over the chairman and the brigadiers themselves.

DOES THE SYSTEM WORK?

We can now summarize the reasons why the kolkhoz system is unable to fulfill its proper function of feeding the country:

(1) It is unable to exploit the productive potential of the land;
(2) It cannot make proper use of the manpower of the countryside;
(3) It drives the educated youth out of the villages, thereby depriving the countryside of the elite which could bring about its reform;
(4) It deprives the peasants of the incentive to work on the land;
(5) It ruins the quality of peasant labor by its exclusive emphasis on quantity;
(6) It is inherently hostile to change, rejecting scientific innovations and the introduction of new equipment;
(7) It leads to the "de-peasantization" of the peasantry by destroying both their incentive and their time-honored habits of work on the land; and
(8) It fosters mutual mistrust and adversarial relations between the managers and the peasantry.

Inevitably the answer to the question "Does the system work?" depends on what one means by "work." If it refers to political control, then the kolkhoz system works very well; if it refers to food production, then the system does not work, for it was not designed to.

Chapter 2

THE GENESIS OF REFORM

DE-STALINIZATION OF THE COUNTRYSIDE

Imagine for a moment that companies of shabashniks like the one Gorin and I observed are introduced as fully autonomous, industrialized units inside the kolkhoz system—instead of working outside it. What would happen then? Would it be just a minor change in the organizational forms, or would it alter the very essence of Soviet agriculture? If the real core of the kolkhoz system is not its collective structure but its *political* function, would not the introduction of the traditional Russian artel' into it change the basic nature of Stalin's invention? In fact, this is what was happening at the time of my conversation with Gorin. A fierce struggle had been raging already for a decade all across the Soviet countryside from Amur[1] to Volgograd,[2] from Omsk[3] to Tashkent[4] to Krasnodar.[5] The artel's being introduced into kolkhozy were called *links* (they resembled only in name the "kolkhoz links" of previous years, which were neither industrialized nor autonomous), and the mass movement connected with them— *Link Reform*. The goal of the movement was precisely to change the function of the agricultural collective from politics, which was alien

[1]See V. Mozhaev, "Zemlia zhdet" [The land is waiting], *Oktiabr'*, 1961, No. 1.

[2]V. Ivanenko in *Komsomol'skaia pravda*, 6/28/69.

[3]P. Rebrin, "Glavnoe zveno" [The main link], *Novyi mir*, 1969, No. 4.

[4]A. Yanov, "Davaite razberemsia" [Let's analyze the matter], *Molodoi kommunist*, 1965, No. 5.

[5]A. Yanov, "Spor s predsedatelem." See also two essays by Vladimir Kokashinskii, one of the most prominent ideologists of the Link Reform—"Nuzhen li selu krest'ianin?" [Does the countryside need the peasant?], in *Propoved' deistviem* [Preaching by action], ed. Kokashinskii (Moscow, 1968), and "Sila v kollektivizme" [The power of collectivism], *Molodoi kommunist*, 1970, No. 2— as well as Iu. Zhukov, "Zveno uspekha" [The link of success], in *Gvardeitsy za rabotoi* [The guardsmen at work], ed. Zhukov, (Nal'chik, 1965).

to it, to the natural one of production. In other words, regardless of what some of the people who supported it might have in mind, the Link Reform was not intended to improve upon Stalin's invention, but to replace it as the main vehicle of agricultural production. Its implementation would amount to what might well be called the de-Stalinization of the Soviet countryside. This was the ultimate message I conveyed to Vasilii Gorin that day in the summer of 1969.

WHO STOOD TO LOSE?

Gorin had several counter-arguments; none of them was ideological. In this sense it was easy to talk to him—as, by the way, it was with the majority of chairmen I met; after all, they were managers, not party professionals. They could be convinced by facts and logic, not by dogmas. Gorin's arguments were very practical, and were reducible in principle to one conclusion: what I proposed was unworkable.

We cannot, he reasoned, model the structure of the kolkhoz on the artel' of shabashniks. The shabashniks arrive and depart, but we live here. Their wages depend solely on their personal labor. It is of no concern to them where the kolkhoz gets money for construction, how construction materials are obtained for them, or whether they build a cow-barn or Roman baths. But we are obliged to know where and how to get money and materials, and to decide how to use them. That's one thing. Then, it's easy to gather an artel' of wandering shabashniks in a large city, one by one, so that there are no personality conflicts. How can you gather such people in a kolkhoz? Third, even if we could gather people for such an artel', how would it work, and how would its wages compare with the wages of other groups—for shabashniks earn three to five times more than kolkhozniks, and you would have to pay the artel' accordingly. The inevitable result would be insults, fights, complaints to the district party committee, anonymous denunciations—in a word, permanent scandal in the kolkhoz. Fourth, would such an artel' be subordinate to our brigadiers, our rules, our discipline, to the kolkhoz charter finally? Wouldn't you get out of it the same sort of alien group as the shabashniks? And if there are several such groups, if they take all the work on themselves, why then a kolkhoz? Won't it then dissolve? And how do you organize relations among the artel's? They don't recognize any language other than money. The entire administrative hierarchy would be disrupted;

the chain of command broken. In order to manage the artel's, you would have to create a kind of a marketplace with market prices for labor and goods. This would be nothing short of a revolution in the countryside. Who would allow it? Have you thought of what the comrades of the district party committee would say? Or what the comrades of the provincial committee would say? Don't you know beforehand what their response would be?

Gorin had immediately seized upon the basic weakness of the proposal around which the reformist thinkers had circled for a whole decade without seeing it. The artel's could not become either a part of the kolkhoz or a subsidiary to the kolkhoz system, as we had long believed. The explosions of conflicts and arguments, from intra-kolkhoz to nationwide, and the outpourings of complaints and denunciations which accompanied attempts at introducing the Link Reform everywhere were by no means contrived or organized in advance, as we had thought. There was an irreconcilable opposition between the artel' and the kolkhoz. The struggles between them were not simply organizational, or even ideological, but essentially political. We should have seen at the beginning what Gorin pointed out ten years later. Perhaps we were too much at the center of the conflict, and in the heat of battle were not prepared for hardheaded analysis.

We should have seen that Stalin's creation—the obsolete kolkhoz system—wouldn't have continued for decades after its creator's demise if powerful vested interests hadn't been behind it. We didn't even think in terms of such special interests—of particular Soviet elites for whom the success of the Link Reform, ultimately undermining the monopoly of the kolkhoz system, would mean the end of the road. Like most Western sovietologists, we thought in rather abstract terms of an undifferentiated "Soviet elite." We spoke of *them* as distinct from *us*, as if they were a unified group, when in fact they were bitterly divided, their interests sometimes in direct conflict. In 1957 Khrushchev was able to crush the elite of the Central Economic Administration only with the support of the provincial elites, the party professionals; when he turned against the elite of the rural party professionals in 1962, he needed the support of the rural managerial elite. Each of these elites hated the others, which is why Gorin immediately thought of the response of the comrades of the district and provincial committees, who had to lose if we were to win. As time has shown, he was right and we were wrong.

25

THE PRICE OF THE REJECTION OF LINKS

However, there was the other side of the coin which, to my knowledge, neither Gorin nor anyone else gave any consideration at the time. Indeed, it became evident only years after the Link Reform had been shelved. It appears that the price for rejecting the artel' (and preserving the monopoly of the kolkhoz system) was immeasurably greater than anyone had anticipated. It had to be paid for by an agricultural disaster which brought with it national disgrace.

I have not seen a more vivid description of the terrible price that was paid than that provided by Viktor Nekipelov—one of the brightest minds of the Soviet dissident movement—in 1979, approximately ten years after my conversation with Gorin:

> The situation in our agriculture seems to be recognized by everyone—from the minister to the kolkhoznik—as being catastrophic.... [But] is the conduct of the economy in our times, and particularly the production of food, the internal affair of one country? Does a country possessing agricultural lands like those of the USSR have a moral right to annually import colossal quantities of foodstuffs, thereby depriving the starving people in the underdeveloped countries in Asia and Africa? By appropriating to itself a significant part of the world food supply the Soviet Union promotes famine in India and in Africa—and in other countries which perhaps have nothing with which to pay for meat and grain.[6] ... It would seem that a country with such agricultural lands should itself feed half the world. But it (with help from abroad!) cannot supply even its own population with meat, butter, milk, and fish. The government of a country which can feed itself and many peoples, and fails to do this out of laziness, sloppy management, and some kind of pathological indifference, is doubly criminal toward its own people and toward the world.[7]

[6]According to some sources, the Soviet "grain raid" of the 1970s on America raised the price of grain on the world market by a factor of three. See for example, Barbara Ward "Another Chance for the North," *Foreign Affairs*, Winter 1980/81, p. 389.

[7]*Kontinent*, 1980, No. 25, p. 171. (On Nekipelov, see "Zaiavlenie A. Sakharova" [A statement by Andrei Sakharov], *Novoe russkoe slovo*, 12/7/80.)

Of course, Nekipelov's passionate indignation is in many respects naive. It is not indifference, and certainly not laziness, which is at the root of the current stagnation of the Soviet countryside. The tremendous energy and power of certain key elites in the Soviet establishment—all their inventiveness and craft and all their political weight—were required to bring the country to such a shameful state. It was not sloppy management, but a political victory of the standpatter provincial elites which led to the result that, in Nekipelov's words, "the money received from the USSR for grain smells of famine in Tanzania or Angola, and smells of the tears of mothers of rachitic children."[8]

When I spoke with Gorin in 1969 the struggle was still continuing, and its outcome was not yet clear. The price which would have to be paid for the rejection of the Link Reform—intolerably high as it was, fraught with national dishonor and, as the events to come would show, with personal disgrace for some, with exile for others, with prison for still others, and even with death for yet others—this tragic price we could not at the time even imagine. And if, for all our political naiveté, we were still able to struggle for a whole decade—and to believe in our eventual victory—the credit for this was not so much ours as that of the winds of rural de-Stalinization which blew over the country in the 1960s, and the spirit of the link movement itself, which appeared to arise spontaneously and invincibly "from below," out of the peasantry itself. The credit belongs to the practical results which the links showed, to the attractiveness and persuasive power of the traditional artel' idea, to the impression of being an "imperative" which it made on many Soviet political leaders. We may say that our struggle was possible because the links working in the kolkhozy seemed like a miracle—the unexpected and immediate cure for an ulcer which had eaten away at the Soviet countryside for decades. It was possible also, as we will see later, because the party professionals as well as the Soviet "priesthood"—the professional ideologists—were acutely demoralized by a series of major political reforms in the first half of the 1960s, and still not firmly in the saddle under the postreformist regime in the second half of the decade. But as the powerful reformist impulse expired, their resistance was growing.

[8]*Ibid.*, p. 172.

THE MOSCOW CONFERENCE

Valentin Popkov, a link leader from the Moscow region, who had nothing to do personally with "high politics," attended a conference in Moscow in the early spring of 1970 where passions boiled over and to speak out was dangerous. No one asked him to speak in the overheated atmosphere of the debates, where it seemed that heads were about to roll. He came and spoke—took a side—and what he said was quite remarkable and deserves to be reported.

Popkov had worked for eighteen years in his kolkhoz as a tractor driver, and during all this time had gathered in harvests which varied between 6 and 8 tsentners of grain per hectare. Since this had always been the case, he assumed it was natural. After all, the land in the Moscow region is the same as in Smolensk—non-Black Earth, poor, not like that of Tambov, let alone that of the Kuban'. In the spring of 1968 he accidentally happened on an article in a newspaper about the links on the Amur, where people who had organized themselves into artels had been able to increase the yield by a factor of two. He showed this article to his colleagues. Several people decided to experiment on their own, hoping to bring the yield up to at least 10-12 tsentners per hectare—a modest enough goal. Popkov's link harvested 60 tsentners per hectare—an unheard of result for these parts. One had only to look at the artless face of this fellow to see that he was not only an honest man, but was himself still somewhat shocked by the miracle which had been accomplished on his fields. Perhaps he expected that everyone in the hall would immediately gasp and then give him an ovation. Instead he heard sinister hints that his figures had been falsified.

Now Popkov was shocked again. He did not understand what was happening in the hall—why these angry men in spectacles so confidently and with so much spite denied what he was reporting. He had never been among so many distinguished and learned people—authors of textbooks, famous names, doctors of sciences. How was he to know that many of these people had devoted their lives to justifying what he was now threatening to destroy with his miracle? How was an innocent village fellow to know that he was in the midst of the "priestly" group of Soviet agriculture, whose dissertations and textbooks had been written to show the superiority of the kolkhoz system over all other systems of agriculture, that they had earned their fame by this and gained their daily bread by it? Would they for anything in the world accept the testimony of an ignorant peasant, which, if it were generally believed, would mean the end of their careers, their status, and their authority?

But Popkov also had defenders at the conference, and many of them were famous too. The most renowned of them was Vladimir Pervitskii, a link leader from the same Kuban' Institute for Testing of Machinery where Aleksandr Erkaev worked. Pervitskii was a valiant warrior of the reform, tempered in many of its battles, and a Hero of Socialist Labor to boot. The accusations which shocked Popkov had been heard by Pervitskii for years, because the miracle which had happened once to Popkov was a regular occurrence for him.

PERVITSKII'S LAND

When I first called upon Pervitskii at the Institute, he immediately proposed an experiment to me: ride out with Erkaev to the field, and I guarantee that you will be able right away to distinguish my land from what isn't mine, even though there are no distinguishing signs on it. He was right. The neatly trimmed, black squares of Pervitskii's land stood out sharply among the kolkhoz fields, luxuriant with weeds. They were like an oasis in a vast desert. This was how Pervitskii demonstrated his theories—experimentally.

Pervitskii had prepared a surprise for the conference where the council of agricultural experts was seeking to discredit Popkov. It was a challenge to the council based upon an experiment he had recently completed. In this instance his experiment had been organized as follows: In the spring of 1969 his link had proposed to the neighboring kolkhoz brigade that they work in direct competition. A kolkhoz field would be equally divided between the link and the brigade, each sowing and cultivating and then gathering the harvest independently, with each side using identical machines, seed, and fertilizer—in all cases obtained from the kolkhoz. Thus all the conditions would be exactly the same, except that on one side of the field there would be nine link members at work, and on the other side, *ninety* kolkhozniks. For the first time in history the artel' threw down the gauntlet to the kolkhoz, and the kolkhoz picked it up. The results of the duel are fully documented in official sources: the kolkhoz half of the field produced sixteen tsentners per hectare; the link half, forty-six.[9]

The angry old men with academic titles could not forgive Pervitskii for the pride with which he pronounced the words, long forgotten in Russia, *my land*—or for his immaculate black squares, or his harvests, or his fame. They wanted to discredit him. He had worked for years in the eye of the storm. For years it had been thrown up to him that, working at the Machinery Testing Institute, he was using the best tractors, special seeds, imported fertilizer. A hurricane of rumors and gossip, the source of which lay suspiciously close to the Institute of Agriculture in Moscow, swirled around him. The essence of the rumors was that he was a plaster hero, created by Soviet propaganda just as in Stalin's time Stakhanov had been created. However, the times were different now, and Pervitskii stood up defending himself.

The most extraordinary phase of Pervitskii's experiment came later, however, when it was time for payment. The kolkhoz paid Pervitskii's link members less than the kolkhozniks—for a harvest almost three times bigger. There was something odd here, but the explanation for it was simple. The kolkhozniks had cultivated—that is, weeded—their half of the field six times (each time poorly), while the link members had weeded their half only once (well). Inasmuch as the work in the kolkhoz was paid for not at an agreed-upon overall amount, as in the artel', but for separate productive operations, the kolkhozniks, who had done more of these operations, received more in payment. "Now tell me,"—Pervitskii asked the council acidly, "why on earth do the kolkhozniks need the harvest?" This was the final blow. The bankruptcy of the kolkhoz system had been demonstrated experimentally: the kolkhozniks indeed did not need the harvest, which portended severe trials for the country if it rejected the alternative which had been offered. But the alternative was rejected.

No one had prodded Pervitskii; no one had required that he throw down a challenge to the powerful "priests"; no one had promised him or his people any rewards in return for their efforts. (In fact, his people lost a great deal of money that summer.) He did what his conscience told him. There are still knights in the Russian land.

[9]A. Yanov, "Zhivaia praktika i konservatizm myshleniia" [Living practice and conservatism of thought], *Literaturnaia gazeta*, 4/8/70.

MY FRIEND IVAN NIKIFOROVICH

The designation "knight of conscience" applies all the more to the most prominent leader and the martyr of the link movement, who paid for his ideas with his life—Ivan Nikiforovich Khudenko. Like Andrey Sakharov, another Russian saint, he had made a successful career in the Soviet system; he was the number two man in the Ministry of Finance of the Kazakh republic—a first-class bookkeeper and accountant, and a quite respectable bureaucrat. But as with Sakharov, he had ideas, and they would not let him rest. In addition, he knew how to infect other people with his ideas: people on all rungs of the social ladder—on the staffs of Politburo members N. Kunaev and F. Kulakov, close associates of Politburo member G. Voronov, and even Nikita Khrushchev himself. But it was not only "at the top" that there were people willing to listen to Khudenko. In three successive experiments over the course of the 1960s, he was able to gather around himself a tightly knit group of sixty who followed him from one end of the republic to the other, believing passionately in him and in his ideas. He was undoubtedly a charismatic leader, my friend Ivan Nikiforovich.

Some of his people had advanced degrees, and among them there were engineers, construction workers, and truck drivers. Many had lived their whole lives in the city but nevertheless went with him to the countryside, to a life they did not know. This was perhaps the only documented case of *reverse migration* in post-Stalin history; people went back to the land not only voluntarily but with enthusiasm. And not for romantic reasons. Khudenko offered them a life full of meaning, and the opportunity to build a new society (on a small scale, of course) according to their own plan and their own values—not those of the higher-ups. The vision of a new kind of social structure was the main thing Khudenko gave them. In this sense, and in the strength of his influence on people, Khudenko was reminiscent of Robert Owen. His ideas also resembled Owen's.

In outward appearance, however, Khudenko rather resembled Khrushchev—the same heavyset body, the same simple peasant face, the same strong dynamism of character and furious temper, and the same hint of adventurism. But intellectually he was quite different from Khrushchev: he thought clearly, and he always knew exactly what he wanted.

He began, as did all kolkhoz leaders who at one time or another were seized by the link fever, with attempts to set up artel's in an ordinary kolkhoz. At the beginning, as in all cases, this went well: the links performed their ususal miracles, but then there began what Gorin predicted and what Khudenko did not foresee—conflicts, complaints, denunciations, and arguments. Then the district party committee intervened, and the reformer was chased out in disgrace (provided that he, like Khudenko, did not wish to retain his post at the price of the dissolution of the links, as most other kolkhoz leaders did in similar circumstances). This was the usual scenario—and essentially what one would expect.

In the first sovkhoz to which Khudenko came, there were 863 workers (two-thirds of whom, as we know, made up the "swamp"), 150 tractors, and a huge number of other machines. Khudenko considered most of these people and this equipment dead weight. In this he differed sharply from the usual chairmen, who are always short of everything. Khudenko dreamed of a fully industrialized and functional enterprise, where for each tractor driver there would be a tractor, and for each truck driver a truck, and, as should be the case in any genuine artel', no surveillance whatsoever—no brigadiers, no agronomists, no economists, no field recordkeepers, accountants, bookkeepers, timekeepers, attendance checkers, cashiers, secretaries, clerks, or, in a word, no chasers of any kind, as well as no horse-and-hand workers.

Very soon he discovered that in order to produce what this sovkhoz usually produced he would need 60 people (six links) with 60 tractors—and that is all. He would not need the usual wage-fund of a million rubles; a quarter of that amount would suffice. It seemed that everything was going well. The links functioned like ideal artel's or "team farmers." They produced twice as much grain as the neighboring kolkhoz brigades, and the cost of production was four times lower than for their neighbors. But something still had to be done with the remaining 803 workers. Whether they worked or not, they still had to be paid. And there were brigadiers and agronomists and field recordkeepers as well who could not be fired. All these people were suddenly left with nothing to do. The machinery also stood idle, deteriorating without use. In addition to all this, the sovkhoz workers could not forgive the link members for all the chaos which had suddenly developed—and especially for their fantastic earnings. In a word, in place of a small revolution there was a huge uproar.

The party officials found Khudenko responsible for the turmoil. He was fired with a reprimand. Someone else might have been dissuaded from any further experiments by such a bitter trial, but Khudenko was as stubborn as Khrushchev and as purposeful as Owen. In addition, he was a Marxist. What had happened to him fit perfectly—at least as he saw it—into the standard Marxist model. New productive forces, revolutionary in their character (the artel's), which were being smothered in outworn relationships of production (the kolkhozy), rebelled and tried to break out into reality. He was not disturbed by the fact that in this case the "new" productive forces were at least several hundred years old, and the "old" relationships of production had existed for only a few decades. It was clear to him that, as had happened in all similar cases in history, the old relationships of production, which had as their agents the party bosses "on top" and the "swamp" of the kolkhoz underneath, were putting up a desperate resistance. Khudenko, of course, saw himself and the other link members as the agents of the new productive forces. It went without saying that in the revolutionary struggle which was under way, the fainthearted ones would capitulate. But Khudenko was not made of such stuff as to surrender after an initial defeat—especially considering that, according to Marx, throughout history the new productive forces have always ultimately triumphed.

Khudenko had lost a battle, but not the war. He prepared for a new campaign. The only problem was to determine what tactical approach to use. He first attempted to transform the links into the industrialized part of the kolkhoz. They were to hold all the machinery in their hands, to have their own land, and to work other land with the machinery for the kolkhoz in return for payment. But the idea of dividing the kolkhoz society into two camps—industrial and backward, haves and havenots, "North" and "South"—was considered offensive and was soon rejected. Khudenko was fired again—with another reprimand. But he knew that he had only to call together the people who had gone through everything with him, and they would come. He could not permit himself to be seen by them as a quitter. It may be that it was precisely this determination—together with his Marxist *Weltanschauung*—which enabled him to bring forward a quite new and this time genuinely revolutionary idea.

In 1968—that is, several years after Khrushchev had been eased out, and the first spontaneous wave of the Link Reform at the beginning of the 1960s had expired with his ouster—a second wave had unexpectedly started rising. This time the Prime Minister of the Russian Federation and a member of the Politburo, G. Voronov, stood behind it. The journal *Novyi mir* endorsed and promoted it, and was joined in the campaign by *Komsomol'skaia pravda, Sovetskaia Rossiia*, and *Literaturnaia gazeta*. The ideological basis for the Link Reform was worked out by a new Institute of Agricultural Economics of the Russian Federation (apparently created by Voronov specifically to confront the priests of the Institute of Agriculture). The idea of the links was supported by the Novosibirsk branch of the Academy of Sciences, including such prominent economists as A. Aganbegian and T. Zaslavskaia, as well as by dozens of journalists, writers, academics, and even some party professionals. In September 1968 the chief theoretical organ of the party—the journal *Kommunist*—spoke out in defense of the links. On May 11, 1969, Voronov, in a most unusual step for a Soviet leader, gave an interview about the links to *Komsomol'-skaia pravda* in which he attacked those who opposed the links. In December of the same year, a great admirer of Khudenko's who was one of the assistants to D. Kunaev, First Secretary of the party Central Committee in Kazakhstan, who is also a Politburo member, managed to insert into a speech by his boss a paragraph attacking the opponents of the links even more severely than Voronov's interview had.[10] The fat was in the fire again, and old Marx seemed to have been proved right. With the backing of at least two Politburo members, the productive forces were finally beginning to overcome the relationships of production.

On this unexpectedly favorable political soil, the seed sown by Khudenko grew. He asked that he and his people be given a piece of desert—a wild place, Akchi, where nobody had ever grown anything— in order to organize (experimentally, of course, and under the supervision of the Scientific Administration of the Ministry of Agriculture of Kazakhstan) "a test farm for the production of grass meal." What he had in mind was high calorie fodder for livestock, of which the republic stood in desperate need. The main crop was to be lucerne. According to Khudenko's plan, his group—the same 60 people as

[10]*Kazakhstanskaia pravda*, 12/25/69.

before—was to handle everything from the plowing of the land and the construction of the settlement to the creation of an automated plant which would process the lucerne into grass meal.

In formal terms, this was an ordinary state farm. But because it was allowed to keep its profits to itself, dividing them among its various artel's, and because it contained not a single horse-and-hand worker or brigadier or agronomist and its management consisted of only two people (who were called members of the "coordinating link"), Khudenko's enterprise was sharply different from anything I had ever seen in the Soviet countryside. It is important to remember this because in it is the key to the paradox which perhaps determined the fate of Khudenko. In their support of Link Reform, *Sovetskaia Rossiia* and *Komsomol'skaia pravda*, Voronov and Kunaev, were talking about *links in kolkhozy*—that is, about what Khudenko had already passed through, and which had already shown its impracticability in the epoch of the first "Khrushchevist" wave of the Link Reform. In the meantime, Khudenko had gone on to carry out something unheard of in Soviet history. It was the first time the reform had really been put into practice.

Khudenko's test farm at Akchi was decisively divorced from the kolkhoz, and appeared as an independent institutional entity—as an alternative to all traditional forms of organization of labor in the Soviet countryside. It was organized completely on an artel' basis. There were 11 links at Akchi. Six of these had charge of field crops; one of materials and equipment (repair and spare parts); one of commercial operations (purchase of seed and fertilizer, sales of finished products to the state); one of construction (of the settlement and the plant); one of public catering (purchase of foodstuffs, cooking); and finally, the coordinating link (more precisely, the Department of External Affairs, which included the director of Akchi—Mikhail Li—and its accountant—Khudenko). The minimum wage was established at 250 rubles a month (compared to 90 in the kolkhozy). The relations between the links were strictly commercial in character—that is, the services they furnished to each other were paid for. For example, the commercial link sold the field-crop links seeds and fertilizer at prices a few percent higher than those at which they purchased them from the state, and their pay came out of this difference. However, the commercial link was concerned about the *quality* of the seed and fertilizer, since the greater the harvest the links received, the higher would be their supplementary pay, which, according to the plan, was supposed to exceed the minimum pay. The same applied to the materials-and-equipment link, which was concerned about the quality of repairs and spare parts. The construction link had to sell the houses it built to the members of the other links; etc.

Thus, exactly as Gorin predicted, market relationships permeated the structure of Akchi. This was, of course, only the first stage of a market economy in Soviet agriculture. For this reason it would be more appropriate to call it a "socialist" market, since it provided only for relations between the artel's, which were not independent entrepreneurs but rather independent economic units within a larger enterprise which handled all the relations with the consumer. In addition, there was no competition between the artel's. On the contrary, they were designed for cooperation, working toward one common goal—to sell to the state as much produce as possible at prices significantly lower than those charged by kolkhozy, which would mean greater profits and higher pay.

Here are the results of the first year's work at Akchi compared to those for a typical kolkhoz, as recorded in official documents.[11] In the kolkhoz the production of one tsentner of grain took from two to five hours; at Akchi it took 25 minutes. The cost of production per tsentner in the kolkhoz was 6 rubles, 38 kopeks; at Akchi it was one ruble, 66 kopeks. The profit per worker in the kolkhoz was 206 rubles; at Akchi, 1570 rubles. The average monthly wage of a kolkhoznik was 88 rubles; the average of a worker at Akchi was 300 rubles.

This was something fundamentally different from the results of Pervitskii's experiment, for all the latter's efficiency. It was something which enabled Khudenko to propose that by separating from the 100 million rural population of the USSR a few million highly skilled workers, and organizing them in enterprises on the Akchi model, the country could reach the average world level of production of agricultural labor, thereby gaining, in place of losses of billions of rubles, a colossal profit. It was in this sense that Akchi constituted a historical event—a kind of micromodel of alternative organization of collective agriculture. And it was by no means a showpiece. It *worked*.

---

[11]V. Kokashinskii, "Chelovek i ekonomika. Eksperiment v Akchi" [The man and the economy. The experiment at Akchi], *Literaturnaia gazeta*, 5/21/69.

It was this which constituted their greatest achievement in the eyes of the participants: in defiance of official procedures, Akchi was a *working* miracle. I heard from Khudenko's people dozens of artless accounts, told with quiet pride. Here is one, which is distinctive only in that it was published:

> Three of my colleagues and I—all engineers with higher education . . . offered to I. N. Khudenko our services. At first it seemed difficult. It immediately became clear that we were not at all trained . . . to make decisions on our own, although three of us previously worked as [chief engineers]. What kind of houses to build? With what materials? What machines to buy?
>
> Now it was solely in our power to decide. . . . We bought—along with the neighboring Burunday sovkhoz—imported machinery for the production of grass meal. The neighbors still have not even tried to use it. With us it works superbly—already for a year and a half. [Unlike the neighbors] we didn't look for an outside contractor. They haven't even filled out all the necessary documents; we immediately started working . . . although violating the established procedures. . . . We invited the most qualified experts on automatic machinery (on weekends), paid them in cash, according not to state norms but how we thought it advantageous. Surely we paid them more then they would earn elsewhere, but our plant is working.[12]

If we formulate briefly the basic implications of the Akchi model, we get something exactly opposite to what we got in formulating the basic features of the kolkhozy:

(1) For the first time since Stalin's collectivization, the Soviet countryside would acquire a coherent professional peasant elite, capable of feeding the country up to a reasonable international standard. This would not require either a gigantic, semi-literate, and amorphous mass of peasants, or a system of total control over them (or, consequently, an immense apparatus for such control). Organized into free unions of "team-farmers," this elite would be self-regulating.

(2) The land turned over to the artel's would come under skilled management capable of fulfilling 100 percent of its productive potential—not 10-25 percent, as in the kolkhozy.

[12]*Literaturnaia gazeta*, 11/18/70.

(3) For the first time since Stalin's collectivization, the countryside would acquire the capacity for a fundamental and permanent modernization. It would be prepared to use the fruits of modern scientific technology, such as high quality machinery and seeds and fertilizers, as well as the services of the most qualified experts in all fields of knowledge—in a word, the new "productive forces" which the kolkhoz system so bitterly resisted. To put it differently, the Soviet countryside in its Akchi model would no longer resist progress.

(4) For the first time since Stalin's collectivization, educated young people would not flee from the land, but on the contrary would seek in the countryside a new role and a new field for the application of their creative abilities.

(5) Finally, the Link Reform would eliminate the adversarial relations between the management (reduced to 3 percent of the working force, in contrast to 40 percent) and the peasantry on which the kolkhoz system is based.

For all these reasons, the Akchi model, if it were to carry the day, would mean the ultimate demise of Stalin's collectivization.

THE RESISTANCE "FROM ABOVE"

The stubbornness with which the Soviet leadership clings to the obsolete and ruinous kolkhoz system is conventionally cited as evidence of the ideological (if not ideocratic) nature of the Soviet state. The struggles of the Link Reform appear to prove, beyond any reasonable doubt, that this stubbornness is political—not ideological. Indeed the Akchi model did not make any attempt to challenge the prevailing ideological prejudices. The kolkhozy could continue to exist by absorbing into themselves the rural "swamp." The only difference would be that they would no longer be responsible for supplying the country with basic food products, which obviously is beyond their capacity. What the kolkhozy would thereafter produce for sale to the state or to private individuals would be an addition—a supplementary means of creating a surplus of food products in the country for internal use or for export to other countries. Furthermore, the Link Reform could be easily justified in terms of the official dogma as a modernization of the form of collective agriculture at a new stage in the development of socialism. The conflicts which inevitably arose under conditions where the kolkhozy and the links existed side by side (such as those which had stopped Vasilii Gorin and had twice led to the collapse of Ivan Khudenko's experiments) would be averted by the separation of the link enterprises from the kolkhozy. Thus the resistance to the Link Reform "from below" might easily be removed. This was what Khudenko hoped for, and he achieved it. It remained necessary to remove the final barrier (which Gorin had foreseen when he asked me "What will the comrades from the district and the provincial committees say?"). In other words, it remained necessary to overcome the resistance "from above."

To be sure, I am far from discounting the ideological resistance. I have noted above with what ferocity the agricultural "priesthood"— the professional ideologues of the kolkhoz system—defended their Stalinist pseudo-scholarship, which was their sole claim to status and privileges. They used their connections "at the top," sowing doubts and suspicions about the ideological purity of the reform. They were not at all squeamish about slandering the personalities of the reformers. People like Khudenko and Erkaev were surrounded by clouds of sinister rumors—as were people like Kokashinskii and me. This made participation in the reform process a perilous business indeed. But these ideologues were a minor threat in comparison with the ominous power of the party professionals—those "heavy-handed, broad-shouldered, square-headed party mechanics" (as Harrison Salisbury once described them). We had beaten the "priests" in public debates, in the press, everywhere we met them. We made fun of them, thinking naively that this was all that was needed to win, but we were mistaken. In reality, as we learned from bitter experience, these were just preliminary skirmishes, just the first line of defense for the anti-reformers. The real fight was yet to come, when the provincial bosses would recover from Khrushchev's devastating blows. Then they would defend ferociously the kolkhoz system—that is, pseudo-production—which represented for them the same thing that pseudo-scholarship represented for the priests: the source of their status and privileges. Even more: for them it was the ultimate justification of their hegemony in the Soviet establishment. From their point of view, the Akchi model of a self-governing union of artel's had one fundamental drawback far outweighing all its benefits: it did not need *them*.

It needed no "fixers" or "chasers" in the form of brigadiers or chairmen, and consequently it did not need anyone to fix or chase the brigadiers and chairmen. In short, with adoption of the Akchi model the comrades from the district and provincial committees become superfluous. It is for this reason that these people who had traditionally referred to culture and agriculture (as distinct from industry) as "party affairs"—that is, as spheres directly subordinate to them—had to enter into a struggle against Akchi, which would represent the beginning of the end of their hegemony.[13]

Certainly, the kolkhozy would remain after the victory of the Link Reform if the Reform were victorious. But if the kolkhozy lost the function, so to speak, of breadwinners for the country, they would remain on the periphery of events; their role would be reduced to a marginal one. Consequently the functions of the people who directed them from their offices would also become marginal. What was at stake for them then was their claim to primary political roles. In the fields of both culture and agriculture, the elites indebted for their survival to Stalinism, which, against the logic of de-Stalinization, continued to dominate in the Soviet establishment, were doomed if the reformist process were to continue. They could not allow themselves the luxury of not intervening to stop it, just as the leaders of the regime of political stagnation in Moscow could not allow themselves the luxury of not intervening in the developing reform process in Czechoslovakia or in Poland. This was a political struggle. We should have foreseen it, and we should have worked out our own strategy for this struggle. We did neither, just as Dubçek and the Czech reformers did not foresee the Soviet invasion and did not work out a strategy for fighting it. Some of us failed to foresee it because of Marxist blinders (e.g., Khudenko), and others because of political naiveté.

THE ROLE OF THE SOVIET PREFECTS

Why the Link Reform failed is the central theme of this book. It is also a subject lesson for anyone involved in any future Soviet

[13]Historically, Soviet industry, due to its technical complexity, was administered by competent specialists—first, after the Civil War, by "bourgeois specialists" (*spetsy*), then by a new generation of engineers. This was never the case in both culture and agriculture, where primacy was given to political control, and direct administration was by party professionals.

agricultural reform to study before starting out on his own thorny path. For this reason alone, the role in the reform process of the provincial bosses—whether we call them party mechanics, as Salisbury does, or Soviet prefects, as Jerry Hough does, or party professionals, as I do—deserves special discussion. There is, however, another reason as well.

At the same time that Gorin was expressing to me his apprehensions that the provincial bosses would never allow the Link Reform, and Khudenko, paying no attention to such warnings, was preparing his final assault on the kolkhoz system in Akchi, a scholarly book by Jerry Hough appeared in America, complete with elaborate appendices and statistical computations, whose primary purpose, it seems, was to rehabilitate these "comrades from the district and provincial committees" by arguing that they represent "the basis for a model of one possible 'modern' political system."[14] As we will see a bit further on, in the ideological war between *Novyi mir* and *Oktiabr'* which split the Soviet literary establishment in the 1960s, the role of the Soviet prefects had been one of the main bones of contention. For the Oktiabrists, who were anti-reform, the provincial bosses were the principal heroes of Soviet literature and society. Accordingly, they glorified these men and their roles as the mainstay of socialism. In his book, Hough appeared to be in agreement with the Oktiabrists, asserting, for example, that "the involvement of the local party organs in the administrative process . . . has been, in large part, a positive, a necessary development rather than a harmful one."[15] The Oktiabrist heroes insisted that the local party organs be seen not as an intrusive element that interferes with the effective operation of the administrative system, but as playing an important role in promoting its effective operation. And it is precisely of this that Hough tried to convince his readers.

Such assertions about the positive role played by local party organs so completely contradict my own experience, as well as that of my friends involved in the reform movement, that I do not dare evaluate them. In the course of my journeys around the country, I had occasion to meet dozens of Soviet prefects on the district level,

[14]Jerry F. Hough, *The Soviet Prefects* (Cambridge, Mass.: Harvard University Press, 1969), p. 317.

[15]*Ibid.*, p. 78.

as well as some on the provincial level, but my experience is a drop in the bucket compared with that of Valentin Ovechkin, one of the founders of the *Novyi mir* party, who spent most of his life traveling around the country and knew most of its provincial bosses personally— or, for that matter, with that of Vsevolod Kochetov, the leading spokesman of the Oktiabrists and author of a novel entitled *The Secretary of the Provincial Committee*. Thus I will give the floor to them and compare the images they present of the character and behavior of the Soviet prefects.

When we analyze both together, a striking result emerges: the Soviet prefects of Ovechkin and Kochetov seem to be antagonists and political adversaries. This is even more striking in that the general theme of both men is the same: the political and cultural crisis of the Soviet society and the corruption of its key elites. The difference is that in one case the source of this corruption is Stalinism—i.e., the dictatorial mode of administration whose principal instruments are the regional dictators—while in the other it seems to be the reforms of de-Stalinization which threaten to destroy the regional dictators.

Ovechkin depicts the Soviet prefects as smothering the initiative of the managers (the leaders of the enterprises) and thereby putting the system into decline. His ideal is a party professional of a new— one might say "Khrushchevist"—type whose intervention into the economic process is limited to the competent selection of managers. Once in place, the managers are allowed to work independently, entering into "horizontal relations" with each other and thereby creating a kind of a self-regulating market system which automatically reconciles their conflicts.

For Kochetov, on the other hand, all this is Khrushchevist heresy. The protagonist of Kochetov's novel, the party professional Denisov, is the absolute and undisputed lord of his province. In contrast to Ovechkin's ideal type, he subordinates work in the economy to the interests of party work. He regulates everything and intervenes in everything. The desire to maximize party controls is the source of his inspiration, his credo, the basic purpose of all his activity:

> In his sleep he is bothered by the same things with which he is busy during the day. He inspects the factories; he rides around the fields. In the factories, the plan is not always properly fulfilled; in the fields, rain hinders the work. In one place someone has strayed

from the party path, and in another there is a shortage of building materials; a scientific institute where the director was poorly chosen is working to no good purpose; more and more children are being born each year, and there are not enough places for them in the nurseries and kindergartens; some foreign tourists are detained on the territory of the military post—what were they doing there with their everpresent cameras? From Borsk and from Drozdov it is reported that for several days there has been no sugar for sale.[16]

On the one hand, "after the recent liquidation of the MTS, not all collective farms have behaved properly,"[17] while on the other, "matters have gotten completely out of hand in the field of literature and art."[18]

The reader may have noticed a certain similarity between the obligations and responsibilities of Kochetov's party professional and those of the Almighty—most clearly suggested with reference to the rain (which, according to Kochetov's portrait, will cease to hinder the work when the first secretary "rides around the fields"). In any case, the first secretary's functions seem to be almost as complex as the Almighty's. They include "the strain of the time of sowing, and waiting for daily reports from the districts, and constant readiness to go wherever a bottleneck or a logjam has occurred—wherever, you assume, matters will not right themselves or proceed in orderly fashion without your [personal] presence."[19]

Of course (we are told by Kochetov), the secretary goes "only where matters are not proceeding, where there are delays, where people can't cope."[20] But—what a strange thing!—it somehow turns out that there is always someone who can't cope with something, or who has run short of something. The builders are short of materials— and building projects stop in their tracks. The agronomists are short

[16]Vsevolod Kochetov, *Sobranie sochinenii* [Collected works] , vol. 4, p. 19.

[17]*Ibid.*, p. 26. MTS stands for Machine Tractor Stations, which were established by Stalin in 1929 for technical servicing of the kolkhozy as well as for political supervision over them. The MTS were abolished by Khrushchev in the course of de-Stalinization.

[18]*Ibid.*, p. 136.

[19]*Ibid.*, p. 69.

[20]*Ibid.*, p. 27.

of essential information—and weeds grow in the fields. The military is lacking in vigilance—and immediately tourists with their "everpresent cameras" appear on the scene. Writers are allowed "to get out of hand"—and rebellious youngsters appear. Provincial cities are short of sugar—and people revolt. Artists are short of critical guidance—and the exhibits are filled with hideous abstractions. Husbands lack fidelity to their wives—and family crises develop. Individual party workers lack devotion to the party—and "comrades stray from the party path." In short, the provincial world under the first secretary's supervision constantly threatens to fall apart. Now he appears to this tottering world in all his might—like a sorcerer, like a *deus ex machina*—correcting everything, smoothing over everything, consoling everyone. Of course to do all this he must be all-seeing and omniscient, competent at once in all matters—agronomic, aesthetic, engineering, moral. He is a regional Olympian. His power can not be a little greater or a little less; it is necessarily absolute, even supernatural. He can not allow himself to appear before his subjects as an ordinary mortal. Who then would believe that he is able to cut through all knots, to resolve all conflicts, to assuage all griefs?

Kochetov's Denisov also appears in Ovechkin's sketches—sometimes under the name of Borzov, first secretary of the district committee, sometimes as Maslennikov, secretary of the provincial committee, and sometimes as Lobov, first secretary of the provincial committee. But these men are not surrounded with the romantic mystery with which Kochetov surrounds his hero, or the halo of infallibility and omniscience so depressingly reminiscent of the halo created at one time around Stalin. Rather the reader finds in them vulgar pretense and petty vanity, horrendous incompetence and crude, high-handed abuse of power, which destroys the initiative of subordinates and creates an intellectual desert. Ovechkin asks:

> Can a party leader of this type inculcate in others, in his associates, the creative boldness of thought, the initiative, the real and not ostentatious efficiency, the principled integrity, which are the most valuable qualities of a person holding a responsible post in the service of the state? . . . In the vicinity of these people, there is not created—let us employ a term from agronomy—a favorable microclimate for the growth and blossoming of talents.[21]

[21]Valentin Ovechkin, *Izbrannoe* [Selected works] (Tashkent, 1965), p. 517.

This kind of party professional "surrounds himself, as though deliberately, with colorless and untalented people as his closest associates"; as a result, "the interests of the state are sacrificed to vanity."[22]

Ovechkin does not deny the effectiveness of these people in carrying out extraordinary concrete actions which require the total mobilization of the efforts of all the participants, such as fighting a war or rebuilding a ruined economy. He is talking about something quite different: in peacetime, when life follows a normal pattern, these first secretaries (who try to create artificially the extraordinary conditions of war mobilization, which is the only justification for their absolute power) are transformed into anachronisms, into antediluvian mammoths who trample down everything around them. He relates how the people in one province joked dolefully about their boss:

> He is the secretary of the provincial committee, and the secretary of the city committee, and the chief agronomist of the province, and the head of all construction projects, and the artistic director of the theater, and the chief architect of the city, and the editor of the provincial newspaper. The only things he hasn't taken charge of are the Young Communist League and the Pioneer Organization: his age won't permit it.[23]

Ovechkin is an eminently practical man. He demonstrates his points with statistics. The inefficiency—the sheer impracticality—of direct control by party organs under ordinary conditions is obvious to him: not only in a huge province but even in a small rural district, where

> there are 20-25 collective farms . . . and 50-60 tractor brigades, and where the collective farms sow 2,000-3,000 hectares. At harvest time, 100-120 combines are working the fields. Even if the secretary of the district committee were to use a helicopter to transport himself around the district, he wouldn't have enough time in the day to stand beside each sower and harvesting combine and check and expedite their work. Even if you sent the entire party staff of the district as "deputies" to the sowing and harvesting units, and

[22]*Ibid.*, pp. 520-21.
[23]*Ibid.*, p. 508.

to gardens and farms and construction sites of collective farms, there still wouldn't be enough personnel to do the job.[24]

And what about provinces where there may be 15, 18, or even 25 such districts? This is why Ovechkin concludes that under ordinary conditions it is impossible to achieve economic efficiency except by "cultivating talented new managers of the economy in the collective farms themselves"[25]—that is, by creating a managerial elite and letting it work according to its ability.

But this is precisely what Kochetov's hero cannot permit. For what does he have left to do where life takes its normal course? Where the peasants sow grain and not weeds? Where the work of factories is controlled by the "socialist market" and by their own managers? Where husbands resolve their conflicts with their wives face-to-face, where books are evaluated by those for whom they are written, and where artists consult their own inspiration for guidance instead of—as in Kochetov's novel—asking the party boss? Here we approach the deepest mystery of the situation of the provincial bosses in the epoch when the national leadership is toying dangerously with reforms. If the reform succeeds, the role of the regional dictators disappears (as, we will see later, was the case under Khrushchev in 1962-1964).

Now perhaps we can begin to understand why—in the heat of a political crisis—the Oktiabrist Kochetov depicts Denisov not only as a positive hero, but also as an almost mystical "personality" around whom there is an aura of infallibility and omnipotence—a "personality cult" on a regional scale. The provincial committee secretary is for him the guardian of the sacred fire of Stalinism—a little Stalin, a regional shadow of the great chieftain.

At the same time we can begin to understand why, for Ovechkin and the Novyimirist critics, both the "priest" (Kochetov) and the prefect (Denisov) are antediluvian mammoths who do not want to die, and who therefore depict the life around them as still abnormal—still, as in Stalin's time, extraordinary. If the priest needs for this purpose "capitalist encirclement" and a "fifth column," then the prefect needs constant bottlenecks, logjams, and shortages. The conflicts

[24]*Ibid.*, p. 512.
[25]*Ibid.*, p. 513.

between supplier and consumer enterprises, interruptions in supplies, deficits, failures, mistakes, scandals, the non-fulfillment of the plan—in a word, everything which the Soviet press calls "temporary difficulties"—all of this is Denisov's daily bread. He needs these temporary difficulties to be *permanent*, for he lives only by the confusion, delays, and basic irrationality of the economic process. Like a vulture, he feeds on carrion. This is why the rule of the little Stalins in the economic process seems to the Novyimirist critics to be just the opposite of what is depicted by Hough in *The Soviet Prefects*. It is a destructive force which leads to a decline in the economy just as inevitably as the rule of "priests" in literature and the arts and sciences leads to their decline.

This, at any rate, is Ovechkin's point of view. My own experience supports Ovechkin. I had an opportunity to discuss the Soviet prefects with hundreds of people who work under their supervision. And in this case my experience was not limited to kolkhoz chairmen and link leaders.[26] I have met many factory directors, their chief engineers, and heads of shops. All of them spoke of the Soviet prefects with passion and agitation as people to whom they were related by profound personal feelings. Never have I sensed so much bile, poison, contempt, and fear in relationships between people in Russia. Only the constant struggle between salespersons and customers in the Soviet Union is comparable in its intensity and fury with the struggle between the middle managerial class and the Soviet prefects. By the early 1960s, when this struggle reached its climax (at least in agriculture, where it resulted in the abolition of the district party committees), Ovechkin's presentation of the prefects seemed much too moderate. We shouldn't forget that he was writing as early as 1952-1954.

In the 1960s it was clear that more than a replacement of one type of prefect by another was required: institutional guarantees were needed against their intervention in agricultural affairs. I admired Khrushchev's actions of 1962 because, for the people whose views I tried to articulate in Moscow, the power of the little Stalins was similar to a plague. No genuine reform stood any chance on Soviet soil as long as their power remained intact.

---

[26]In *Detente After Brezhnev* I have described in detail a meeting with a director-general of a huge productive association (pp. 22-27).

And for this reason I have to disagree with Hough, who presents the Soviet prefects as a necessary and positive element "of one possible 'modern' political system." To be sure, Ovechkin and I may be mistaken, and Kochetov and his priests may be right. It may be that their resistance to the reformist process in general, and the de-Stalinization of Soviet agriculture in particular, is fully justified by some higher principle unknown to me rather than solely by their selfish group interest. If so, why does not Hough articulate this higher principle? Why not analyze the argument between the Novyimirist and the Oktiabrist parties in such a way as to show that the anti-reformist priests—and their allies, the Soviet prefects—were right in their bitter fight with the reformist party? The Soviet system is not static; it has its own dynamic; it develops. It was the attitude of Hough's heroes toward economic, managerial, and ultimately political change which was challenged by *Novyi mir.* There was plenty of material in the Soviet press exposing the Soviet prefects as the core of the status quo or stand-patter party in the Soviet system opposing the reforms. In other words, a thorough scholarly work on the Soviet prefects requires an explicit argument with *Novyi mir.* Indeed one has to be fully cognizant of the arguments of the reformist party if one is to provide effective scholarly ammunition for the Oktiabrist party and to bless its unholy alliance with the little Stalins.

Now let us look a little more closely at how the prefects supervised agriculture in the times preceding the Link Reform and the Akchi model—and how they continue to supervise it now after the reformists have been defeated.

THE LITTLE KHRUSHCHEVS VS. THE LITTLE STALINS

I will for the most part quote from Ovechkin here, and reduce my own comments to a minimum, because he succeeds so well in giving the reader the flavor of life in the Soviet provincial "upper reaches" and of the everyday behavior of the little Stalins in their milieu. Here is his account of a Soviet prefect, a first secretary of a provincial committee:

Having seen much of life, having a pretty good understanding of people, and taking a somewhat cold and skeptical attitude toward the people around him, he did not like flatterers and sycophants and made fun of them, but he did not tolerate at all those who were *not* toadies, and not "quiet ones"—workers with good heads on their shoulders and independent views about things, who sometimes even tried to raise an objection about something. In the course of time the number of competent workers on the staff of the provincial committee and in the other provincial institutions declined. Either they were forced to request transfer to some other province, or they were sent "by agreement" to ministries or administrative offices. The staff positions which were vacated were inevitably occupied by people who, taking account of the unfortunate experience of their predecessors, didn't dare to contradict the secretary of the provincial committee, Lobov, in anything, and kept themselves "lower than the grass and quieter than water." Lobov . . . took a hostile and contemptuous attitude toward "fence-straddlers" who changed their convictions and "scientific theories" seven times a week; nevertheless, these people settled themselves comfortably around him, and even increased in numbers. By his intolerance of any difference of opinion, Lobov developed around himself that "servility" which he sometimes inveighed against at meetings of the executive committee or plenums of the provincial committee.[27]

It is clear that the style of leadership of an upwardly mobile Soviet prefect as described by Ovechkin could not help but lead to numerous conflicts in his staff. Ovechkin provides an example of one such conflict:

The head of urban services, in a fit of bureaucratic zeal and eager beaverism, paved over part of the lane in which Lobov had his residence—from the main thoroughfare to the secretary's villa and a few meters beyond—just enough for the ZIS[28] to turn around on the pavement. The remaining hundred yards of the lane, up to the next paved street, remained without asphalt and full of potholes. Lobov, returning from vacation and seeing in front of his house such a thoroughly "krokodilic" instance of fawning behavior, became indignant, called the unfortunate road builder before the

[27]Ovechkin, pp. 517-18.

[28]ZIS is the abbreviation for Zavod imeni Stalina—the Stalin automobile plant in Moscow. The ZIS was the official Soviet government limousine in the 1950s.

provincial committee, heaped the most extreme abuse on him, and compelled him within 24 hours to pave over the rest of the lane. He later referred to this case at sessions of the city and provincial soviets. Nevertheless, this [head of urban services] remained in his post, and did not even receive a reprimand. However, when the deputy chairman of the provincial executive committee in charge of construction—a good worker, a careful man, a deserving and well-regarded person in the town, and the commander of a partisan detachment during the war—had a big argument with Lobov, . . . carried his case to Moscow, and obtained reconsideration of plans which had been approved in the provincial committee, he paid for it by being transferred to the post of director of a state reserve in the forest-steppe region.[29]

As we can see, neither past services nor prestige and a high position in the town could save the prefect's subordinate from political annihilation.

Another example of a conflict described by Ovechkin is even more vivid:

Metelkin, the head of the provincial weather bureau, in following a strict order not to give weather predictions to the districts which had not been approved by the provincial committee . . . went so far as to bring only those predictions to the provincial committee which Lobov would have liked to have. If the provincial committee had taken a decision to increase the sown acreage in a certain crop, Metelkin would make a prediction implying that the weather for sowing and growth of that crop during the spring months would be the most favorable possible. If telegrams went out from the provincial committee to the districts calling for the immediate beginning of sowing of millet and buckwheat, Metelkin, paying no attention to the cold weather or even to the frost, would predict a sharp rise in temperature in the next few days. If there was talk in the provincial committee that it was necessary this year to begin the sugar beet harvest earlier than usual, . . . Metelkin would affirm the necessity of these measures by promising an early and very rainy autumn.[30]

[29]Ovechkin, pp. 518-19.

[30]Ibid., p. 519.

Of course, Metelkin could not guarantee his forecasts. The kolkhozy immediately began the sowing of millet and buckwheat—and the frosts just as immediately killed the crop. The kolkhozy expanded the sowing of this or that crop or began the sugar beet harvest earlier than usual, and they had to sow the crop over again, or they lost the sugar because the beets were not ripe. This was an unconscionable swindle. Let us not forget, however, that all these decisions were made by the provincial committee *before* Metelkin provided his false predictions. Let us also not forget that Metelkin was strictly forbidden to give weather predictions to the districts which had not been approved by the provincial committee. In other words, the provincial committee—which is to say, Lobov—determined the periods of sowing and the periods of harvesting of all agricultural crops, whether millet, buckwheat, or beets, and it also determined the weather forecasts. Metelkin merely endorsed its decisions, so to speak, with the authority of science. And the belief in the legitimacy of such manipulation of agriculture, and even of the weather, is so deeply ingrained in the minds of the party professionals, that even such a bold and honest observer as Ovechkin, who had spent most of his life in close contact with these people, is struck not by the overall manipulation, but only by the falsification of the weather reports. For all my sympathy for Ovechkin, I must note that he, who hated Lobov, had nevertheless lost his capacity to be astonished by the unnatural character of Lobov's behavior, and was shocked only by Metelkin's.

This then is how the administration of agriculture as a party affair looks in practice. Consider for a moment the contempt for the peasantry and for peasant labor and the idiotic self-confidence with which it is permeated. Should we be surprised, after this, at the cynicism of the brigadiers and tractor drivers?

However, let us return to Lobov. Since the reader is now familiar with his type of behavior, he will certainly not be surprised that Lobov chastised the falsifier Metelkin, christened him "provincial champion in servility," and made a laughing-stock of him, but of course *left him in his post.* At the same time,

Chekanov, the head of the agricultural administration, who was not satisfied with the role of rural data gatherer for the provincial committee, and tried to work out certain new questions of kolkhoz production, ... *did not last long in his post.* He worked with Lobov for only half a year. At the first opportunity he was detailed to a neighboring province.[31]

Ovechkin does not venture beyond a psychological explanation of this phenomenon:

> Perhaps it was out of jealousy of anyone else's authority that he [Lobov] could not tolerate the presence next to him of clear-headed people and unusually talented organizers. Or was there a cold indifference in the depths of his soul to the matters over which he had charge? It was a matter of complete indifference to him who would be in his post after him if he were transferred to another place.... "Let the grass not grow after me. Let even Metelkin be named head of the agricultural administration of the provincial committee."[32]

In depicting the psychology of a Soviet prefect—his weakness for incompetent intriguers (Metelkins), his jealousy of competent managers (Chekanovs), and the intellectual vacuum which develops around him as a result—Ovechkin leaves no stone in place of the shrine of party professionalism erected for us in the Oktiabrist literature. The most intriguing thing in his sketch, however, is something else.

It would seem that we understand well the inevitable result of Lobov's administration: the Chekanovs are destined to vanish into political oblivion one after the other, and their place will be taken by Metelkins—until his milieu will be made up solely of Metelkins, who will transform themselves into Lobovs when their chance to rule comes. This analogy of the inevitable transmission of power from Lobovs to Lobovs could be applied to the imperial Lobov himself: Joseph Stalin, who also formed his entourage with his own Metelkins—i.e., with future Stalins. The analogy *has* been used with reference to Leonid Brezhnev. But for some reason, contrary to the seemingly implacable logic of Lobovism, among the many Metelkins in Stalin's entourage, there emerged the indomitable reformer Nikita Khrushchev, who nourished in himself hatred both for Stalin and for his autocratic style of administration. The process of creation of these, so to speak, little Khrushchevs on the provincial level—in the milieu

[31]*Ibid.*, pp. 519-20. (Emphasis added.)
[32]*Ibid.*, p. 520.

and in the entourage of the provincial little Stalins—is for me the most interesting thing in Ovechkin's work. Life turns out to be more complicated than straight-line logic, and in place of the Chekanovs who go docilely into the shadows by the will of the autocrat, there come other people with the capability and daring to challenge his unlimited power. In practice there take place—at the same time and parallel to each other—two opposing processes: the growth, so to speak, of the dictatorial potential of the Soviet prefects, and the growth of the reformist potential of some of their subordinates. Inevitably the two processes and the people who embody them collide, and conflicts arise.

One cannot help noticing that Ovechkin himself is quite unaware of the complexity of the process he describes. Like all of the Soviet neo-Marxists of the post-totalitarian era—like Khrushchev and, a decade later, Khudenko—Ovechkin was completely dominated by the view that history is unilinear and following a rising curve. In conflicts and battles along the thorny road, the ascendant class of warm-hearted Chekanovs are breaking the backs of the Lobovs and moving toward victory—so the future looks to them. A romantic belief in the power of reason is ingrained in these people—an unshakable conviction that the side opposing reason is fated to lose.

Let us see how Ovechkin describes a conflict between a typical warm-hearted Chekanov—Petr Martynov, a former journalist and chairman of a kolkhoz who has been promoted to the secretary of the district committee—and Maslennikov, the second secretary of the provincial committee, on a personnel question. Martynov proposes that a certain Medvedev (an analogue of the Metelkin we know about) be discharged from the post of secretary of the district committee, and an experienced manager Dolgushin (an analogue of Chekanov) be named in his place. Maslennikov naturally objects. Martynov—in the presence of the first secretary of the provincial committee—responds as follows, exposing the deepest, darkest secrets of the Stalinist hierarchical vertical principle:

"Birds of a feather flock together! You hate Dolgushin, but support Medvedev, because you yourself are Medvedev! You're the same kind of fixer and chaser as he! The mental capacities of the Medvedevs suit you perfectly. They know how to yell at people, and that's all. And you don't demand anything more, because

that's the limit of your organizational abilities. . . . You need pup-
pets in the district, not living people with minds and hearts. . . .
You like to have people in the district who eat up everything
you say, and like parrots repeat after you word for word without
thinking. You hate Dolgushin precisely because he is not a puppet,
but a living person. He is a talented manager; . . . but it's not for
you, of course, to judge the talents of others because you are yourself without talent."[33]

Note that in this burst of indignation Martynov is not challenging
the Soviet prefect himself—only the second secretary of the provincial
committee, the shadow of the boss, who incidentally is a great man
in the province and perhaps the prefect of tomorrow. A direct challenge to the prefect himself on the part of a subordinate is taboo in
Soviet literature: it was taboo before Ovechkin's time and remains so
today. But before Ovechkin's time such a devastating characterization
of a party professional of the rank of provincial secretary was abso-
lutely unthinkable. And if we bear in mind that Ovechkin is describing
not a fictional confrontation, but a clash between living people, the
impression made by Martynov's speech is a strong one. There is little
basis for the triumphant optimism which creeps into Martynov's tone,
but Ovechkin's hero is confident of the future. He continues his de-
nunciation:

"You are acting mean right now because you feel that a bad time
is approaching for you! Executives are facing complicated tasks.
One can't rely on general commands and yelling, and you can't
administer in any other way. There is nothing more to be gotten
out of you. That is all of which you are capable. How you will
adapt yourself to other methods I don't know—and you don't
know. And you can't adapt yourself: it isn't within your capabilities. You are in bad shape."[34]

In fact, what Martynov assumes as a postulate—that the increasing complexity of the economic and administrative mechanism
will in and of itself end the dictatorship of the Lobovs, necessitating
a revolution in personnel and the replacement of the intriguers by

[33]*Ibid.*, p. 479.
[34]*Ibid.*

new managers—is only a hypothesis. This is not enough for victory. There is also required a sophisticated political strategy for squeezing out the Metelkins and the Lobovs. Unfortunately, as we now know, the little Khrushchevs did not understand this, just as their patron and inspiration, the real Khrushchev, did not. Therefore they, not the Lobovs, were doomed to lose the game. If Martynov had listened more attentively to the response the Soviet prefect made to his diatribe, he would perhaps have felt the chill of defeat long before it actually came:

> "Here you have called [the secretary of the provincial committee] a fixer and a chaser. I know his value and do not overestimate his talents. But remember that *such people are still necessary in the provincial committee....* Unfortunately we still have in the province quite a few secretaries of district committees who need chasers. Do you think we can quit reminding people like them of such obvious truths as that beets have to be dug up promptly or you lose half the harvest, that a day lost in harvest time costs many thousand tons of grain, or that fallow fields have to be plowed in May and not in July? If you do, you are mistaken: you have to remind them and remind them. For instance, right now, we have to dig many trenches for the summer to hold the mass of soilage which we have obtained. All over the place there are grown-up people sitting as secretaries of district committees who know that soilage isn't cured in barrels, like sauerkraut, and that if we don't prepare the trenches by the beginning of the soilage harvest, our whole strategy for a fodder base for our livestock goes to pot. Do you think that if we leave them to their own devices, if we don't press, if we don't give orders, and don't threaten punishment, we will have trenches? Assurances and promises—that's what we'll have, but not trenches. You don't know our personnel! There are secretaries of district committees ... who begin to shake a leg only when they receive a warning or a reprimand. Someone has to follow along behind them with a club, and explain to them that ... tractors have to be repaired, that plowing has to be done to a certain depth, that fallow fields that have grown up to weeds have to be plowed. No, brother, we still need fixers and chasers! Don't be an idealist."[35]

[35] *Ibid.*, pp. 480-82. (Emphasis added.)

All this is said benevolently, patiently, quietly—and a complete picture of the party affair gradually spreads out before us. But it seems that we have already seen it—at another time and in another place. Doesn't the brigadier in the kolkhoz "follow along . . . with a club" behind the tractor driver, "reminding, giving orders, and threatening punishment" if the ground "is not plowed to a certain depth"? The surprise element in the response of the Soviet prefect is that the provincial committee secretary has the same attitude toward his district committee secretaries as the kolkhoz brigadier has toward his tractor drivers.

Here the circle is closed, coming to an ultimate absurdity. There are in the country only a few thousand rural districts and sixteen million party members. Can't there be found among them a few thousand talented managers? But talented managers don't administer rural districts for the same reason that there are no educated brigadiers in the kolkhozy. The system of total surveillance repels them, just as it repels the kolkhoz youth, science, and new technology. If you replace the little Stalins or Medvedevs with Chekanov-style managers, or even little Khrushchevs-Martynovs, the system will quickly force them through a reverse transformation. The Chekanovs will be transformed into Medvedevs, and the little Khrushchevs into little Stalins. For the "club" in the kolkhoz system is inevitable. The moment the brigadier puts it down, "our whole strategy," to use the prefect's words, "goes to pot" in the brigade. At the moment Lobov puts it down, the whole province and the whole country "goes to pot." The beets will not be dug up, the fallow fields will not be plowed, and the soilage will be cured in barrels like sauerkraut. The whole system is bound by a vicious circle, the symbol of which is the club in the hands of the higher authorities.

Here then is the deeply hidden truth, not reflected in any official document, on which the power of the Soviet prefects in the countryside rests. This is how they think of themselves—quite sincerely: the countryside will nourish the country as long as they carry it on their shoulders the way Atlas carries the earth. And the most terrible thing about this is that they are right. The kolkhoz countryside, an invention of Stalin, the artificial fruit of dictatorship and the result of the destruction of the peasant elite, really cannot be left to its own devices. For it will cease to work (even as badly as it works now) as soon as the club is laid down. Faced with this merciless truth, all the speeches of the little Khrushchevs-Martynovs—like those of their great patron who headed the party and the government—are claptrap in the eyes of a prefect.

That is why Martynov was wrong in addressing the secretary of the provincial committee with the grim words of warning "You're in bad shape." No *Mene mene tekel upharsin* will light up on the walls of the Soviet temple for the Soviet prefects as long as the kolkhoz system, into which, as we have seen, they have put down their deepest roots, still exists. And as long as the little Khrushchevs-Martynovs don't go beyond personnel changes into a basic revision of the system itself, their quixotic optimism sounds irritatingly naive. Even with a very highly developed political imagination, it is almost impossible to conceive, as Martynov did, that the prefects who earned their black caviar along with their Olympian status precisely as fixers and chasers will voluntarily renounce all this even if the welfare of the nation is at stake.

THE SCOPE OF THE PROBLEM

But we were politically naive. As one by one the prefects withdrew their support for the links, we tried to figure out the personal motives in each case. We sought to explain their actions by indifference, by infirmity, by meanness, by stupidity—in a word, psychologically—as Ovechkin did before us, and as Nekipelov is doing now. Even the coincidence of their actions did not lead us to suspect the truth. The notion that there might be a strong consensus or a group interest—that this is what politics is all about—did not enter our minds. But how could we suspect such a thing? Growing up in a uniform, seemingly apolitical society, locked up from the outside world, where were we to get the notion that there were group interests? That these interests might oppose each other? That what awaited us was not friendly collaboration, but harsh confrontation with the upper reaches of the establishment? Even after a decade of struggle, when we understood the enormous physical (so to speak) scope of the problem, its political dimension kept escaping us. On the surface it looked as if not the Soviet prefects but the kolkhoz society itself was mounting the resistance to the Link Reform— that it was coming primarily from the middle (the apparatus of the kolkhoz administration) and the lower (the kolkhoz "swamp") levels. [36]

In a striking scene presented in *Novyi mir*, P. Rebrin, one of the ideologists of the Link Reform, shows us the middle level resistance:

I remember the spacious hall of the district committee of the party, almost full of people. On the dais, there was first [the link leader] Polevoda, then [the district committee secretary] Nikonov. In the hall there was the "middle echelon" [brigadiers], agronomists, bookkeepers, accountants. . . . The district committee secretary addressed them. But strangely the faces of all those sitting in the hall seemed to be stamped from one mold—inscrutably indifferent and slightly condescending. Figures showing the excellent results achieved by the [links] were cited, and the hall was silent! Comments were asked for concerning the prospects for development of the new method, and the hall was silent! [37]

We have already encountered a similar situation, haven't we? Although what Rebrin described took place in Omsk province in eastern Siberia, thousands of kilometers from Belgorod, where the kolkhoz chairman Vasilii Gorin addressed his tractor drivers, the reaction of the audience to the speeches was the same stone wall of silence. Nevertheless, there is a difference—and it is fundamental. In Belgorod, the chairman of an ordinary kolkhoz, supported by the middle echelon, tried without result to fire the enthusiasm of the kolkhozniks, whereas in Omsk, a link leader, supported by the secretary of the district committee, tried to fire the enthusiasm of the middle echelon. Rebrin continues:

Ten minutes later, [Polevoda] said to Nikonov in his office: "I understand, Valentin Ivanovich, why there was silence. It is very simple. If, let us say, they allow in our kolkhoz ten such [links] as ours, then almost all of this army which was sitting in the hall will be unnecessary. We will not have to be administered."

And this is how the secretary of the district committee—an exact copy of Ovechkin's Martynov—answered the link leader: " 'Look: we have eight sovkhozy, eight thousand workers and clerical personnel.

[36]For discussion of the "swamp," see pages 8-11 above.

[37]*Novyi mir*, 1969, No. 4, p. 159.

Only 3,920 participate directly in production: the rest are all servicing the others. . . . How would there not be higher costs of production? Under the [link] system, all this would swiftly decline.' "[38]

The reader, who is familiar with Khudenko's experiments, will see right away that this Martynov here repeats the error of Khudenko's first experiment. For of the 3,920 who are alleged to participate in production, the vast majority are not needed. According to Khudenko's later calculations, eight sovkhozy need only 480 people to maintain full production—and certainly not the eight thousand that they have now. Even if we assume that the conditions of Omsk province require different calculations than those on which Khudenko based his figures, the difference will still be immense.

Polevoda had in his link five equipment operators and two shepherds. At their disposal were 200 head of livestock, 630 hectares of plow land, and one grazing pasture. In addition, they shared one livestock barn, three tractors, and two combines. This was all that was needed for each link member to yield a product (in meat and grain) worth 9,900 rubles (compared to 2,000-2,800 rubles produced by one tractor driver in a kolkhoz brigade in the Omsk province), while earning 344 rubles per month (as against 100 rubles for a kolkhoz tractor driver). If ten such links are needed in the sovkhoz, according to Polevoda's calculations, then for 8 sovkhozy only 560 people would be enough. The question arises: what is to be done with the other 7,440 who live in the sovkhozy, who have to be paid and cannot be discharged? There obviously is the potential for a demographic collision there—a very serious one, in fact unsurmountable in the context of the kolkhoz system. Only the Akchi model, which called for a total separation of independent link enterprises from the kolkhozy, and a policy of "peaceful coexistence" between the two—could solve the problem. Yet neither Polevoda in his provincial backwater, nor his advocate Rebrin, nor their high-level patrons in the Politburo— Voronov and Kunaev—suspected that this potential for a demographic collision could be used as a political weapon to destroy the reform.

It is clear that not even the physical scope of the agriculture problem, let alone its political scope, was properly understood by the majority of people who launched the Link Reform—beginning with the tractor drivers on up to the most sophisticated Martynovs. Like

[38]*Ibid.*

all revolutionaries, we were full of hope, arrogant and enthusiastic but terribly ignorant—even at the end of the 1960s, after a decade of struggle.

THE FIRST WAVE

We were all the more ignorant at the beginning, when the Link Reform suddenly roared from east to west like a forest fire, not decreed by anyone—out of the Amur region into Omsk province, from there into Altai territory, then into Kazakhstan, and finally into the north Caucasus and the Ukraine, the main breadbaskets of the country. As far as one can judge, something like approval of the reform at the highest level was first sounded at the January Plenum in 1961 when Khrushchev declared: "The facelessness of the earth must be terminated; the field must have its master."[39] But considerably before this, in the fall of 1959, family links appeared on the Amur, and the villages were immediately filled with rumors about the miracles they were accomplishing.

The main crops in the Soviet Far East are soybeans and potatoes.[40] The link members there doubled the soybean harvest—and sometimes significantly more. In 1961, in the neighboring Khabarovsk territory, the kolkhozy gathered harvests of 2-3 tsentners of soybeans per hectare; the link members along the Amur gathered in 11-13 tsentners per hectare.[41] The difference was dramatic. What Pervitskii had conceived as an experiment in Krasnodar took place in Khabarovsk of its own accord at every step. In the Border Guard sovkhoz, 167 brigade tractor drivers and 27 link members were working in two neighboring fields. The amount of land to be worked by each group was identical—2,700 hectares in wheat. Each tractor-brigade member harvested 90 tsentners; each link member, 1,100 tsentners. In other words, one link member produced as much as 12 brigade tractor drivers.[42] The difference was even more striking than in the Pervitskii

[39]Quoted from *Oktiabr'*, 1961, No. 4, p. 190.

[40]In Russia, "Far East" refers to the region fronting on the Sea of Japan—the Amur province and Khabarovsk territory—together with the island of Sakhalin.

[41]*Oktiabr'*, 1961, No. 1, p. 132.

[42]*Ibid.*, p. 137.

experiment, even though no national figure stood behind these links. Furthermore, the Amur link members could not, like Pervitskii, be accused of holding privileged positions.

In the case of soybeans, an ideologist of the link movement on the Amur, a sort of Far Eastern Martynov—Iosif Shtarberg—calculated that each link member was able to produce 645 tsentners, whereas each brigade tractor driver produced only 145 tsentners. The most interesting result, however, involved potatoes. The average potato harvest in the kolkhoz field had never exceeded 60 tsentners per hectare. Before the introduction of the family links, no one had paid much attention to the fact that the kolkhoz families produced 3½ times more potatoes on their private plots than in the kolkhoz fields. This difference was duly noted, however, as soon as these families had link land assigned to them—that is, when the artel' principle was applied not only to the private plots but to the collective land as well. Each family worked at its link land as a team from beginning to end and was awarded all the profits from it. The harvest yield leaped up as though by magic—by a factor of precisely 3½![43] For the first time since Stalin's collectivization, the gulf between the productivity of collective and private land, which had always seemed unbridgeable, was bridged. What the kolkhozy for decades had not been able to do—and still are not able to do, and never will be able to do—had been done by the links in one year.

It should come as no surprise, then, that after the writer Boris Mozhaev visited the Amur in 1960, he composed a rapturous paean to the Link Reform. The journal *Oktiabr'*, where Mozhaev's ecstatic hymn of praise was published, was literally snowed under with letters from readers.[44] Although the general tone of the response was full of

[43]*Ibid.*, pp. 128-29.

[44]*Oktiabr'*, 1961, No. 4, p. 184. The reader might well wonder why it was the anti-reformist *Oktiabr'* that allowed Mozhaev's essay (and the subsequent discussion) to appear in its pages in 1961. However, *Oktiabr's* anti-reform stance took shape gradually during the 1960s, and the pattern of its formation was complex and convoluted. At the first stage of the debate (1961-1964), following the line of their allies (the little Stalins) and in the heat of the establishment crisis, the Oktiabrists tended to see the root of evil not so much in reform as in Khrushchev personally, who was a patron of their opponents—the Novyimirists. It was only at the second stage of the debate, in the period of the post-reformist regime, that their eyes were opened to the dangers of reform as such. It was at this point

enthusiasm, the first doubts were also sounded. The family structure of the links was criticized, for example. Readers pointed out that in the family links people had to work 16-17 hours a day, and that the family fields were not sufficiently large to provide for full crop rotation. Furthermore, the family system did not address the problem of full mechanization of agriculture. For that matter, not everyone has a family able to work regularly in the fields. In short, Mozhaev's strong sympathies for the family links did not persuade all his readers. The readers concluded that the family link system could not become universal, and what they wanted was precisely something that could be universal. So great was the readers' enthusiasm for a universal link system that, strange as it may seem, they (as well as Mozhaev) overlooked the potential for a demographic confrontation, which was destined to become a major tool in the fight against the links.

The readers from the Hammer and Sickle kolkhoz of Kharkov province wrote that, having read Mozhaev's article, they immediately divided up all the kolkhoz land and saw for themselves that most of the one thousand people who usually worked in the fields were really not needed there.

> We have calculated that we will be able to get by with only 150-200 people in the fields, [and that is] if we do not buy machines by spring. . . . If we can get the machines we need, then only 25-40 people, and no more, will be needed in the kolkhoz for basic jobs.[45]

The question of what was to be done with the other 950-975 workers was not even mentioned. Mozhaev's contacts on the Amur spoke with similar enthusiasm about the prospective demographic effects of the reform. One of them even developed a plan for the elimination of the village as a social phenomenon:

> One can't build an agricultural city if 200 people are cultivating 1,000 hectares. . . . It is another matter if 20 people are working in place of an entire kolkhoz. The assignment of land [to the links] will free thousands upon thousands of working hands for us. And where a large village now stands, there will be a light field camp

that the links were purged, so to speak, from the pages of *Oktiabr'*, finding refuge in *Novyi mir*.

[45] *Ibid.*, p. 185.

with two or three cottages. The people will live in real cities. And, brother, will they live well![46]

Still another Martynov! A kind of national euphoria really did prevail at the beginning of the Link Reform, with no ideological objections being voiced.

Thus the links spread of their own accord like grass, with a kind of wild spontaneity—a genuine mass movement, performing miracles of productivity and conquering even the hardened hearts of the kolkhoz autocrats. All this took place without directives from the party, without a noisy campaign in the newspapers, without organized leadership—in a completely un-Soviet way. When Mozhaev inquired of one of the link leaders who the initiators of the reform in the kolkhoz had been, he received the following answer: "What kind of initiators are you referring to? Go ask any peasant, and he will give you the same answer! We gathered at the administration building, talked about it, and decided to assign all the potatoes and corn to the links."[47] This would appear to indicate that the kolkhoz chairmen were working hand in hand with their people in this brief period of euphoria up to 1964. The usual adversarial relations between the management and the peasantry seemed to evaporate in the kolkhozy that adopted the link system, and the entire spirit of the work on the land changed.

More important, the organizational forms of the links developed spontaneously:

(1) They started out as family teams, combining industrial and manual labor. (The husband was a tractor driver, while the wife, the elders, and the children were manual workers.) Then they abandoned the family principle and grew into artel'-type organizations, fully industrialized.

(2) They began specializing in one crop. Then they transformed themselves into "universal" units, working vast fields with a full crop-rotation cycle.

(3) They combined animal husbandry with crop-raising.

As Khudenko's Akchi clearly indicates, they were capable of developing even further—of completely divorcing themselves from the kolkhozy and creating a genuinely alternative form of agricultural organization.

[46]*Ibid.*, 1961, No. 1, p. 137.   [47]*Ibid.*, p. 128.

The links were indeed a living experiment, continually adjusting to the complexities of modern agriculture, and in the process indicating the way in which the Soviet countryside would develop if it were allowed to develop naturally. They appeared to offer the solution to the seemingly insoluble problem of Soviet agriculture, hopelessly trapped between the obsolete kolkhoz system and the ideological impossibility of a return to private farming.

By 1963 there were more than 2,000 links on the Amur, and 5,000 in the Altai territory;[48] in the Kuban', there were 3,000 according to one source, and 5,350 according to another;[49] in the Ukraine, there were 30,000.[50] By 1965 there was nothing—or almost nothing—left of them. For example, one of the most articulate advocates of the Link Reform, Anatolii Strelianyi, later reported in *Novyi mir*: "After October 1964, almost all of the Kuban' links broke up—some in form and substance, and others only in substance."[51] As the reader well knows, October 1964 was the end of the Khrushchev era—the end of the regime of Reform. This is why I have called the first, euphoric and spontaneous wave of the Link Reform "Khrushchevian."

THE THREE LEVELS OF CONFLICT

When I went to the Kuban' in the summer of 1968 to do some research on the causes of the disintegration of the links, many of the kolkhoz chairmen showed by their manner that they did not want to waste precious working time (and for kolkhoz chairmen all time is working time) discussing the links—a stillborn notion, as they now saw it.[52] If I nevertheless succeeded in starting up a discussion about it, their objections were no longer organizational or technological, as in 1961; they were chiefly ideological. They insisted that it is not the Soviet way of doing things to go back after half a century of socialist

[48] I. G. Shtarberg, *Kompleksnye mekhanizirovannye brigady i zven'ia* [Complex mechanized brigades and links] (Blagoveshchensk, 1963), p. 72.

[49] See Yanov, "Dispute with the Chairman," and Shtarberg, p. 172.

[50] Shtarberg, p. 172.

[51] A. Strelianyi, "Zveno v tsepi" [A link in the chain], *Novyi mir*, 1969, No. 4, p. 171.

[52] See the beginning of "Dispute with the Chairman."

kolkhoz farming to individual private production, to private owner-
ship of the land, essentially to capitalist farming, covered only by a
fig leaf of collectivism. And they cited examples of link failures—
examples which at first glance seemed to prove their point beyond
question.

Consider this example provided by one of the chairmen:

The brigade's land, on the crest of the hill, has dried out early, and
is ready for plowing, while on the link land, in the middle of the
valley, everything is still wet. The link tractors are standing idle,
and they will stand idle for several days more. Is this right? But if
you try to order our "team-farmers" to plow that kolkhoz hill,
they won't listen. It's not their land; let it go to hell. On their own
land they will wear themselves out, working 12 hours a day if need
be (which, incidentally, is a violation of the labor laws), as ignorant
peasants toiled on their own land under the tsar. You can't tear
them away from that land; it is as though it were truly their own
heritage and property. You wouldn't believe it: they guard it and
put watchmen on it at night, when the harvest is ready, in case—
God forbid—someone should drag away a corn-cob or a truck
should run over the field. But the kolkhoz land is literally alien to
them; they simply don't care about it. Isn't this the approach of
private farmers? And this is only the beginning. What takes the
cake is that they exploit hired labor—that is, they act not only like
private farmers, but like kulaks, bloodsuckers, bloody capitalists.
Where any manual labor is needed, they are not about to bend their
backs. For this they hire kolkhoz women. And they pay them according to the norm, as it's done in the kolkhoz, by the penny, and
they themselves receive according to the contract, quite handsome-
ly. Isnt't this kulakism? Listen to what our women say about them:
the old times of the kulaks have returned. In some villages there
have almost been mutinies against these links. There is no arguing
the fact that their labor productivity is high, but so is it among the
farmers in America. What are we to do now—return to capitalism?

I had countless similar conversations in the Kuban' in 1968 with
the chairmen who had driven away the links. But I did not recognize
these chairmen. It seemed that they had completely lost their peasant
common sense, for which they had always been known—that they
were saying things overheard from or suggested by others. It seemed

that priests and party professionals, the trash from the provincial committees, were speaking through them. From the peasant point of view, all this was obvious nonsense. P. Rebrin in *Novyi mir*—as I did in *Literaturnaia gazeta*—analyzed all their arguments in detail in order to show that all of them were rubbish. Here I will repeat only the essence of our analysis.

Conflicts about the links usually arose on one of three levels: (1) between the tractor drivers who worked in the links and those who remained in the kolkhoz brigades; (2) between the link members and the management of the kolkhoz; (3) between the link members and the kolkhoz "swamp." The source of the conflict between tractor drivers is almost always the enormous discrepancies in payment for growing various crops. There are prestige crops, and there are plebeian crops. In the Kuban', say, wheat is ranked high by comparison with sugar beets. In the period when the links were expanding rapidly, and everyone was enchanted with them, the links were given the prestige crops, as well as the best machines and fertilizer, which inevitably put them at odds with the other tractor drivers. Where one tractor driver gets 100 rubles, and another—of the same level of skill and for the same amount of work—gets 400, conflicts are unavoidable. They could be settled in two different ways. One was to intensify the reform—that is, to include all the tractor drivers in the links. This was the path that Khudenko followed. The other way was to liquidate the reform—together with the high labor productivity and the abundance of goods it promised. In other words, throw out the baby with the bathwater. This was the path the majority of kolkhoz chairmen followed after October 1964.

Resolving the conflicts between the link members and the kolkhozy management also presented no particular difficulties. One had only to set up (as Gorin envisaged) commercial "market" relations among the links and the management, and there would be no problem in persuading, let us say, the link situated in the valley to plow the land on the hill. The only thing required would be to pay the links according to *their* rate. Even simpler would be to give the hill to a link. Khudenko took this path, but after October 1964 the majority of chairmen took the opposite one.

The conflict between the link members and the "swamp" could be removed in an even simpler way. If, for example, the ground is so overgrown with weeds that kolkhoz women have to be brought in to weed it, why shouldn't these women be paid by contract just as the link members are—that is, with a share of the profit? What would there be to fight about then?

It's almost impossible to believe that the kolkhoz chairmen didn't understand that their arguments were nonsense.

THE CHALLENGE AND THE RESPONSE

But if, understanding the absurdity of their criticisms, they suddenly began to speak in ideological clichés, what could this mean? To compare their "party" speeches at the end of the 1960s with their "managerial" speeches from the Khrushchev period, full of concern for the land, was to see what a long distance—intellectually—these chairmen had traveled in a decade. Here is an excerpt from the managerial speeches made at the beginning of the 1960s:

> Yes, we have to assign the land. . . . Today Ivan scratches it, tomorrow Fedor, and the next day Sidor. . . . And the grass grows, and no one is responsible for it. . . . The earth is a living organism! It feeds us, and we must be responsible for every single piece of it—personally responsible.[53]

If all the age-old peasant canniness, all the managerial ability of the chairmen suddenly seemed to vanish, it could mean only one thing: the constructive solutions of the three types of conflicts which arose in the kolkhozy in connection with the Link Reform had to be perceived by them as the beginning of the end of the whole kolkhoz "game." The lessons of the first wave of reform were understood as spelling death for the kolkhoz autocracy, and it became clear that if, first, all the land was assigned to the links and, second, the relations between the links became commercial and, third, there was no more need for the subsidiary labor of the kolkhoz "swamp," then the metamorphosis of the Soviet countryside would have been complete. The kolkhoz system would have been transformed into the Akchi model. Khudenko's experiment showed that this was the logical next step in the Link Reform. We have to conclude that the sudden ideological shift in the speeches of the chairmen arose from the fact that they

[53]Quoted by Mozhaev in *Oktiabr'*, 1961, No. 1, p. 131.

had looked into the abyss and drawn back from it in fright. In the old days the peasant would have crossed himself and prayed in order to scare away the specter of the devil; in the Soviet time he began to spout ideological incantations.

We can now see that in the short five-year period of its existence—from the appearance of the first family links on the Amur in the fall of 1959, to the dramatic end of the Khrushchev era in the fall of 1964—the Soviet countryside passed through a course somewhat analogous to what it passed through during the NEP period from the spring of 1921 to the fall of 1929.[54] Just as the development of private initiative in the 1920s led to a differentiation within the peasantry between a productive elite and a rural "swamp," which confronted the leadership with a fundamental political choice, so the Link Reform in the first half of the 1960s led to an analogous differentiation and a similar need for a political choice. The Stalinist leadership of 1929 replied to the challenge of peasant differentiation by liquidating NEP and instituting forced collectivization. The post-Khrushchev leadership replied to the challenge by suppressing the Link Reform and restoring the status quo.

Of course this analogy should not be pushed too far. In the 1920s the kolkhoz system had just been created—in the mud and blood of terror and civil war in the countryside. In the 1960s, the long-established system resisted the destruction of the Stalinist legacy. However, in both cases the response to peasant differentiation was counterreformist.

WHY THE REFORM WAS ALLOWED TO HAPPEN

Now, when we can see quite clearly the magnitude of the changes the Link Reform would have brought to the kolkhoz coun-

---

[54]NEP—New Economic Policy—is the name given to a complex of measures introduced by the Soviet government in 1921 which resulted in a partial restoration of agricultural enterprises employing hired labor. (The number of workers permitted was limited, and goods could be sold on the free market only under certain conditions.) However, the NEP had political significance far exceeding this purely economic description. As became obvious immediately after its termination, NEP represented a political alternative to a dictatorial regime accompanied by total terror, purges, and a Gulag. In Soviet parlance, NEP spells relief—both political and economic.

tryside, and consequently, the intensity of the resistance which it necessarily evoked, there is no reason to ask why the overthrow of Khrushchev proved to be a defeat for the first wave of reform. It is more reasonable to ask: Why had reform been allowed to go so far? Why was it not smothered in the cradle before it could demonstrate results so threatening to the kolkhoz system? Where were the priests with their ideological clichés before October 1964? Why did not the little Stalins with their dictatorial power immediately suppress the Link Reform, which clearly deprived them of the very meaning of their existence as Atlases who carried the Soviet countryside on their shoulders?

It is clear that the middle echelon—the administrative apparatus of the kolkhoz—was the first to sense the potential threat of the reform. It was this group—the paid staff—which would be the first victim of the metamorphosis of the Soviet countryside. Under the Akchi model there was nothing for it to do. There could hardly be any doubt that the middle echelon had to seek allies—both below (in the kolkhoz swamp) and above (among the Soviet prefects). There is no doubt either that it was they who set the swamp against the link members, thereby provoking continuing conflicts on which the chairmen then seized as a pretext for breaking up the links. They also must have appealed to the party professionals. If all these elements of the resistance had been able to move against the links as a united front, we probably never would have heard of Khudenko or of the experiments of Pervitskii in the Kuban', Valentin Tiupko in Central Asia, Nikolai Manukovskii in the Voronezh area, Aleksandr Gitalov in the Ukraine, and Aleksei Dugintsov on the Amur. Such people as Kokashinskii, Erkaev, Shtarberg, Mozhaev, Strelianyi, and Rebrin would not have become spokesmen of the link movement. None of this would have happened had a united front against the links developed in the Khrushchev era. Why didn't it develop?

The answer to this question seems to me to be of primary importance. Our notion of the conditions under which the differentiation of the Soviet countryside developed without hindrance up to October 1964, and perhaps could have succeeded beyond that, depends on this. In this sense, the first wave of the Link Reform, with its unanswered questions, was a kind of seductive historical experiment. It seems rather foolish to let it simply pass into Lethe without an attempt to find the answer. For this we will have to transfer our attention for a while from the links to the high politics of reform. But before we do this, let me advance a hypothesis: it would seem that a united front of resistance to the first wave of the Link Reform did not develop because the Soviet prefects—its main political force—were paralyzed by their own problems. One might say that they were waging a struggle for their political survival.

Chapter 3

THE POLITICS OF REFORM

THE "SOVIET WATERGATE"

Khrushchev's relations with the Soviet provincial elites were complex. They trusted him because he, unlike Malenkov, was one of them: a peasant son who climbed the ladder of the provincial hierarchy—from the secretary of district committee, to the provincial committee . . . all the way to the top. He was their inspiration; he symbolized their pattern of success. Khrushchev, on the other hand, trusted them. They were his people; he led them in the Kremlin revolt of June 1957 against the oligarchy; they raised him to power. Once in power, its exercise apparently seemed to him quite simple. Like Ovechkin, the chronicler of the failings of Soviet prefects, Khrushchev believed in the miraculous virtues of socialism. What Ovechkin thought of Lobov, Khrushchev must have thought of Stalin: the old scoundrel crippled a wonderful system for the sake of his personal vanity. Let's get rid of the Lobovs and their dictatorial heritage, preached Ovechkin, and the system will perform miracles. Khrushchev, a former Lobov himself, must have reasoned the same way: by getting rid of Stalin's dictatorial heritage, we are letting the system work. He believed that a Soviet economic miracle was in the making; like the rest of us he was full of hope and politically naive. As early as 1954 he was convinced that "the opening up of the virgin lands will [not only] give us the possibility of fully satisfying our demands for grain, [but also] we will be able to export grain to the capitalist countries."[1] In 1958 he declared that the USSR would in three years overtake the United States in the production of meat and milk, and

---

[1]N. S. Khrushchev, *Stroitel'stvo kommunizma v SSSR i razvitie sel'skogo khoziaistva* [The building of communism in the USSR and the development of agriculture] (Moscow, 1963), vol. 1, p. 303.

he also expressed confidence that "the time will soon come when the state will buy grain [only] from those collective farms which will sell it at a cheaper price."[2]

This euphoric vision was brutally undermined when, in 1960, competition with the United States in production of meat and milk ended not with the anticipated triumph, but with a huge scandal in which his former allies, the Soviet prefects, played the primary role. The first secretary of the Riazan' provincial committee, Larionov, who reported overtaking U.S. production levels in his province by increasing the output of meat and milk by a factor of three, for which he was awarded the Golden Star of the Hero of Socialist Labor, turned out to be a fraud. The "overtaking" was a gigantic hoax. Not only were the Riazan's kolkhozy completely stripped, but additional meat and milk had been bought from neighboring provinces. As a result, Larionov was dismissed and shot himself, and his story became a symbol of the corruption of Soviet prefects and signalled the beginning of what I call the "Soviet Watergate"—i.e., a general purge of corrupt party professionals. The Larionov affair turned out to be just the tip of the iceberg: exposures of the corruption of the little Stalins followed rapidly one after the other, sometimes reaching staggering proportions. The highest leadership of the Tadzhik republic—Ul'dzhabaev, first secretary of the republican party committee; Obnosov, second in command; Dodkhudoev, the republican premier—had all, it appeared, long been engaged in the same kind of fraud Larionov was involved in. In the words of Frol Kozlov, the second in command under Khrushchev and one of the speakers at the 22nd party congress:

> They implanted . . . toadyism and bootlicking, violated party democracy, and broke the law of the state. . . . Finding themselves unable to provide for further development of the economy of the republic, [they] resorted to fraudulent acts. . . . They resorted to eyewash and false reporting. The state plan for the procurement of cotton was not fulfilled in the republic, but its leadership, having lost all shame and conscience, reported that it had been fulfilled ahead of time.[3]

[2]*Ibid.*, vol. 3, p. 207.

[3]*XXII S'ezd Kommunisticheskoi Partii Sovetskogo Soiuza. Stenograficheskii otchet* [The 22nd Congress of CPSU. Stenographic report] (Moscow, 1962), vol. 3, p. 14.

As these public exposures indicated, at this point Khrushchev had to acknowledge something the Novyimirist party had been saying all along: his former allies were swindlers; they were little Stalins whose power was destructive. But the most humiliating thing to face was that, in addition to all this, they often behaved stupidly. The first secretary of the Artashat district committee of the Armenian republic, for example, ordered the entire press run of an issue of a district newspaper taken out of circulation and destroyed when he didn't like its editorial. In another instance, the first secretary of the Sergokalinsk district committee of Dagestan republic responded to his critics by declaring: "No tsar ever gave up his power voluntarily, and I don't intend to give mine up without a fight."[4]

For Khrushchev, however, the worst thing about the Soviet prefects was that they were incompetent and ineffective. Just as the "little Khrushchev" Martynov put it in Ovechkin's sketch: they relied on general commands and yelling in their administration because they couldn't govern in any other way.Their ability to manage agriculture was very limited; they were fixers and chasers. The only thing they could do well was follow the kolkhoz chairmen with a club. One can't get an economic miracle out of that kind of management.

What Khrushchev should have realized as early as 1960 was that in the business of economic modernization the Soviet prefects were his enemies, not his allies. As Ovechkin had explained years before, they were part and parcel of the Stalinist heritage which the country had to get rid of in order to move ahead. The remedy Khrushchev came up with originally was the same as Ovechkin's: replace the little Stalins with little Khrushchev-Martynovs. But Khrushchev soon understood that Ovechkin's remedy would not work, and he would later attempt, in effect, to destroy his former allies-turned-enemies. Instead, they destroyed him. But this final outcome shouldn't distract us from our effort to reconstruct the politics of reform.

At first, Khrushchev's severe disillusionment with his former allies was reflected in a purge of regional dictators unprecedented in its proportions in the post-totalitarian era. In 1960-1961 more than half of the first secretaries of provincial committees in the Russian republic and in the Ukraine (57 of 101) were discharged. Almost two-thirds of the members of the "parliament" which had brought

[4]*Ibid.*, pp. 9, 10.

THE POLITICS OF REFORM

Khrushchev to power in June 1957 fell victim to the Soviet Watergate: only 37 percent of them were reelected to the Plenum of the Central Committee in October 1961. The journal *Kommunist* wrote in somewhat veiled form of people whom

> Comrade N. S. Khrushchev sharply criticized [and] in particular of the leaders of Tula, Kirov, and Riazan' provinces and of the Ukrainian SSR. . . . These are not political organizers but careerists, people who wormed their way into the party; they bring shame on the party and must be expelled from the party and turned over to the law. . . . Our party has at its disposal a large reserve of personnel, and we must boldly embark on the replacement of the officeholders whose positions are now bankrupt.[5]

This last remark must have been the most ominous the party professionals had heard since Stalin's death. It was a declaration of war against them. In this context, the announcement that there would be a dramatic new reduction of the Soviet armed forces hardly seemed coincidental.

This Soviet Watergate marked, as I see it, the beginning of an establishment crisis in Moscow—that is, a more or less open conflict between the National Leadership and its original power base—its former allies, the "parliamentary" majority which brought it to power, the Soviet prefects, the military, and the Soviet priests. From that point on, the issue became who would get whom first: either the National Leadership would succeed in creating a new reformist power base, or its former allies would oust it before that could be achieved.

THE DE-STALINIZATION FORMULA

At the January Plenum of 1961, Khrushchev was already attempting to establish the legitimacy of his conflict with the "parliamentary" majority by bringing about a revision of the party "general line" under which he had come to the helm four years earlier. Undoubtedly his strongest attack was directed against the military-industrial complex. Here we encounter for the first time

[5]*Kommunist*, 1961, no. 2, pp. 8-9.

what I call the "de-Stalinization formula," which was to become the nucleus of Soviet Protestantism.[6]

"In the first period of Soviet power," said Khrushchev, then adding, in order to identify the period specifically with Stalinism, "in the years of the first five-year plans,"

> we directed all our efforts to creating heavy industry, . . . which, as we know, is the basis of the defensive capability of the country. We were compelled to do this in order to ward off the imperialists. We built socialism under conditions where our country was encircled by a hostile capitalist environment. In order to survive . . . we devoted all our strength to the creation of heavy industry.[7]

Compare this Khrushchevian analysis with what Malenkov had said in defense of the Stalinist general line:

> We know that our party began industrialization with the development of heavy industry. . . . The acceptance [of the proposal of the "capitulationists" to shift resources from heavy to light industry] would have meant the downfall of the revolution, . . . since we would find ourselves disarmed in the face of the capitalist encirclement.[8]

As we can see, the analysis of the victor corresponds almost word for word to that of the vanquished. Khrushchev continued:

> Now we have an entirely different situation. . . . Our economy is in the full flower of its strength. The defense of the Soviet country is sound. . . . The Soviet Union is not the only socialist country. . . . Our capabilities to fulfill the needs of the people have grown immeasurably. . . . We cannot [any longer] permit lagging development in agriculture and in industry producing consumer goods.[9]

Here is what Malenkov said on this subject: "Our country now has a powerful heavy industry. . . . Now, on the basis of what has been

[6]See Notes on Terminology, pp. 127-30 below.

[7]Khrushchev, vol. 4., p. 287.

[8]*Kommunist*, 1953, no. 12, pp. 14-15.

[9]Khrushchev, vol. 4, pp. 288-89.

achieved, we have all the conditions for organizing a sharp rise in the production of consumer goods."[10] Again, the correspondence is almost verbatim.

But while he repeats what Malenkov said, Khrushchev goes further in his political analysis of the situation by seeking to identify the forces hostile to increased production of consumer goods—i.e., to the post-totalitarian concordat with the consumer:

> I understand that some of our comrades have developed a hunger for metal. . . . But if a great deal of metal is produced and other branches are allowed to lag behind . . . this will lead to a one-sided development. . . . The prosperity of the state is determined by the quantity of products man receives and consumes . . . and the degree of satisfaction of all his needs. . . . Therefore, we should not behave like the flounder, which can see in only one direction.[11]

The moment the leader of an autocratic system, one of whose distinguishing characteristics over the decades has been the assumption that mass consumer interests are secondary relative to the power of the state, refers to the people who are occupied in expanding this power as "flounders"—this moment can justly be considered the official inauguration of Soviet Protestantism. Nine months later he would address the people with "a hunger for metal" even more sharply, accusing them of wearing "steel blinders," and of not knowing how to do anything except shout "Steel! Steel!"[12] He would declare in London that "Soviet heavy industry has been built. In the future, light and heavy industry will be developed at the same pace."[13] And he would continue this thought in Moscow: "We will now reduce the expenditures on defense . . . and direct this money into the production of mineral fertilizers."[14]

It was not only that the leader of the Reform publicly preferred mineral fertilizers to the glorious Soviet military: he also attacked the priests—"hidebound dogmatists"—in an attempt to finally depoliticize

[10]*Kommunist*, 1953, no. 12, p. 15.

[11]Khrushchev, vol. 4, p. 290.

[12]*Ibid.*, vol. 7, p. 362.

[13]*New York Times*, 5/21/61.

[14]Khrushchev, vol. 8, p. 51.

the very issue of the general line. In 1964, on the eve of his downfall, he would say:

> The program for chemicalization of the economy takes in both the sphere of production and that of consumption, and it cannot be said that it relates only to group B or group A. One thing is indisputable: the chemical industry synthesizes the interests of the state in the development of heavy industry [and] the interests of the Soviet people in the rapid increase of the production of consumer goods. . . . Only hidebound dogmatists can see in this a deviation from the general line. . . . There can now be no counterposing of group A and group B.[15]

What eleven years previously had sounded in Malenkov's mouth like a manifesto of de-Stalinization, signaling the birth of a concordat with the consumer, and what nine years previously had sounded like the greatest political heresy, "capitulationism," and even "a slander on our party," was now glorified as the newest wisdom of that same party. To anyone who has read the speeches of Soviet leaders, it is quite clear that both for Malenkov and for Khrushchev, this was not merely a tactical step. It was a formulation of a fundamentally new strategy. It was a philosophical-historical formula, diametrically opposed to the general line and the whole philosophy of Stalinism. The essential feature of this schema was its division of Soviet history. into two distinct epochs from which followed two fundamentally different strategies. The first epoch was the period of the first five-year plans and of capitalist encirclement, when in order to survive it was necessary to sacrifice the welfare of the people to create heavy industry as the foundation of the defense of the country. The second epoch was the period of Reform, when the defense of the country was sound, Russia was no longer a fortress surrounded by enemies, and therefore the duty of its government was to concentrate on satisfying the needs of the people. In this formula, the philosophy of consumerism and peaceful coexistence was contrasted to the ascetic and isolationist philosophy of Stalinism.

This formula incorporated everything achieved by the Russian reformers in the first period of the Reform—1953-1960. It implied

[15]*Ibid.*, pp. 449-50, 451.

77

that its initial stages had been completed: the old dictatorial regime
had been destroyed, and the new post-totalitarian society installed.[16]
The time had come to stabilize it. The way was open for comprehensive economic reform as well as general liberalization, for which the
formula provided the philosophical foundation. The whole complex
of dramatic events, revelations, and institutional changes which followed Stalin's death and is included in what is termed *de-Stalinization*—the end of the regime of dictatorship and of control of the
establishment by the political police, the elimination of mass terror
and slave labor, the ouster of the post-dictatorial oligarchy and the
institutionalization of the Soviet "parliament," the rehabilitation of
millions of innocent people who had been arrested and imprisoned
on false charges, the relaxation of censorship, the introduction of
Soviet Protestantism and the concordat with the consumer, the ideological split in the literary establishment between the reformist *Novyi
mir* party and the anti-reform *Oktiabr'* party, the end of the total
domination of the economy by the military-industrial complex, and
the collapse of the Central Economic Administration in May 1957—
turned out to be not the end of the road, but the first step toward a
new civilization, if you will, which had shaken the dust of Stalinism
off its feet once and for all. As in all previous Russian Reforms, the
moment of truth had come. Philosophically, the needed steps had
been taken. Would the National Leadership be able to meet the political challenge?

The Link Reform could serve as a litmus test. If the National
Leadership, which had lost confidence in the Soviet prefects' ability
to achieve an agricultural miracle, was looking for a new power base,
it was waiting in the wings. Indeed, if in the whole history of post-
Stalin Russia, there was a moment when—politically speaking—the
possibility of institutionalizing agricultural reform looked bright, it
was at this moment of Khrushchev's attack on his former allies—the
moment of the Soviet Watergate. It was then he had the opportunity
to replace those in the "parliament" whom *Kommunist* described as
"bankrupt" with the leaders of the reform—people like Khudenko,
Erkaev, Pervitskii, and Shtarberg—who, along with other representatives of the middle managerial class, could create a strong link
caucus able to provide the political protection badly needed by the

[16]See Notes on Terminology, pp. 131-34 below.

developing mass reformist movement. Here was Khrushchev's chance to become a Russian Kadar.

BACKWARDS INTO THE FUTURE

I would find it very hard to believe that Khrushchev had a carefully planned, comprehensive political strategy which he sought to realize in a series of actions. I am inclined to agree with Edward Crankshaw that he "moved backwards into the future,"[17] and that like virtually all the well-known reform leaders in imperial Russia, he was not a "coherent policy maker"[18] of the type of Bismarck, or Cavour, or even Ivan III, Great Prince of Muscovy, who tried to turn Rus' (not yet an empire in his time) into a European state at the end of the fifteenth century.[19] It is enough to recall some of his many political blunders: the Berlin Wall and the Cuban Missile Crisis; the senseless attack on the private plots and personal livestock of collective farmers; the manifestly illegal persecution of believers; the reckless utopian promises; the attacks on liberal writers and artists and the patronage of the scientific impostor Lysenko; the attempt to destroy the grassland system of agriculture; the notorious corn campaign; and a great deal else which helped to consolidate his enemies against him and repel his allies—both within the country and in the world. He caused his people much grief and did many absurd things. In the final analysis, Khrushchev was a graduate of the Stalinist academy of total terror, and in a sense we should be surprised less at his cruelties, which seem rather natural, than at the many good deeds he was able to perform despite his terrible past.

It seems to me, however, that we should be even more surprised at the fact that he still moved into the future, even though "backwards" and "incoherently"—that his instincts led him in the right direction, and that he was brave enough to throw a desperately bold challenge in the name of the Russian consumer to his own constituencies.

The crisis created by Khrushchev during 1960-1964 was different from the Hungarian and Polish crises of 1956. In Hungary and

[17]*Khrushchev: A Career* (New York: The Viking Press, 1966), p. 270.

[18]*Ibid.*, p. 272.

[19]See my *The Origins of Autocracy*, pt. 2: "The Absolutist Century."

Poland, it was a question of conflicts between the regime and the society-at-large, whereas the 1960-1964 crisis in the USSR involved a conflict between the National Leadership and the "parliamentary" majority. In order to explain this peculiar "establishment crisis" (as I call it) in an autocratic system, let us adopt, for argument's sake, Alfred Meyer's suggestion to regard the Soviet system as a gigantic corporation.[20] Let us assume that a limited number of the largest shareholders of the USSR, Inc. (in this case the provincial elites, the "priesthood," and the military-industrial complex) hold a controlling interest, thereby dominating the board of directors (the National Leadership). In general it may be said that the holders of the controlling interest would attempt to replace the president of the company in two situations: (1) when they came up against an open rebellion by the mass of stockholders (as occurred in Hungary and Poland), or (2) if they thought that the president's policies threatened their own interests (the equivalent of the establishment crisis we are talking about).

The fall of Khrushchev in October 1964 is a good example of the latter situation. In fact, the overall economic and food supply situation in the country was better then than at the beginning of the 1980s, when there was economic stagnation and chronic food shortages. The conflict between the regime and the society was not as sharply defined as in the 1970s—at least there was no cold war against the intelligentsia and no dissident movement (which doesn't mean that there were not individual dissidents). Most important, there was hope that the country was "on the rise"—hope which does not exist anymore. Why then did Khrushchev fall? Nothing threatened Brezhnev until the end, despite the fact that his energy had fallen off markedly, while Khrushchev—full of plans and energy—was brought down. Here, perhaps, we come up against one of the most profound characteristics of the post-totalitarian society: the sociopolitical situation in the country may in some important instances undermine the leader indirectly, through the situation in the political establishment. Even in a relatively favorable sociopolitical situation, the leader may fall if he comes into an irreconcilable conflict with the "parliamentary" majority, and an establishment crisis arises as a result. On the other hand, even a clearly unfavorable situation in the

[20]"USSR, Incorporated," in *The Development of the USSR: An Exchange of Views*, ed. Donald W. Treadgold (Seattle, 1964).

country may not significantly influence the leader's position if an establishment crisis is prevented. Or, to put it differently, a rebellion of the population, such as occurred in 1956 in Hungary, or an open split in the ruling party, like the one in Czechoslovakia in 1968, are not the only kinds of major political crises that can happen in a post-totalitarian society. There can also be the kind of crisis which developed in 1960-1964 in Moscow with Khrushchev's across-the-board challenge to the largest shareholders of USSR, Inc. and the Soviet Watergate, with the revival of Malenkov's de-Stalinization formula and the attempted revision of the general line, with the rapidly growing link movement undermining the power of the party professionals in the countryside, and the ideological split in the literary establishment threatening the power of the "priestly" hierarchy in the field of culture, with the reduction of military expenditures and the declaration of war against the "steel-eaters," undercutting the power of the military-industrial complex. During the four-year period, the political scales tilted both ways: sometimes it seemed that Khrushchev was retreating before the pressure of his opponents, and sometimes that he would succeed in breaking their resistance.

One of the most delicate questions which arises at this point concerns the position of the West in relation to this establishment crisis. Which of the contending parties had the West's political support—the conservative elites, whose victory almost certainly foreshadowed political stagnation within the Soviet Union and an accelerating arms race in the world arena, or reformist Russia, broadly understood, including not only Alexander Tvardovskii and *Novyi mir*, but also Ivan Khudenko and the Link Reform and even Nikita Khrushchev and his war on "steel-eaters"—that is, the whole reformist potential of the post-totalitarian society, whose victory might have led to comprehensive economic reform, reduction of the armed forces, and general liberalization of the regime? The arms race of the 1970s could perhaps have been averted if the West had tried to influence the unfolding crisis in order to at least make it harder for the conservative elites to win. Unfortunately, there appears to be no way to answer this question; it seems that hardly anyone in the West thought that the West should take a position in this crisis. The professional politicians are hardly to blame, if it was not regarded at the time as a political crisis of major proportions even by professional sovietologists. At least I don't know of anyone who in 1960-1964 clearly articulated the view that the pace of the arms race depended on the outcome of this crisis, or that the huge Soviet arms buildup may not have taken place if reformist Russia had won its struggle.

"A HAREBRAINED SCHEME"

I do not mean by this that the sovietologists did not discuss such significant events in Moscow as, say, the adoption of the new party constitution (bylaws) in 1961, or the liquidation of the rural district committees of the party and their replacement by production directorates, or the bifurcation of the provincial committees of the party into independent rural and urban committees in 1962. Nor do I deny that a great many perceptive observations and remarkable intuitions concerning the personal and factional fights in the Kremlin at this time can be found in the works of such prominent kremlinologists as Michel Tatu, Carl Linden, Sidney Ploss, or William Conyngham. Given the unusually open (by Soviet standards) debates of the Khrushchev period, the Kremlin watch was indeed in its heyday during those fateful years of the establishment crisis. What I am saying is that these events were not put together with the ideological war between *Oktiabr'* and *Novyi mir*, the growing Link Reform, the rebirth of the "de-Stalinization formula," and the purge of party professionals, etc., into a single picture of a major political crisis—of a decisive battle of "Russia vs. Russia."

For example, J. W. Cleary in his survey of sovietological views concerning the reforms pointed out that

> Almost without exception it is held that at least in agriculture, if not also in industry, the party [as a result of 1962 reforms] has been strengthened at the expense of the state apparatus. . . . It has even been suggested that the party will become so engrossed in production matters that it will be utterly depoliticized and, in effect, transformed into the principal agency of national economic administration."[21]

[21]"The Parts of the Party," *Problems of Communism*, July-August 1964, p. 55. The author uses phrasings such as "From the wealth of comments by Western observers . . . there has emerged a general consensus. . . ." and "Discernible in recent literature is a measure of agreement. . . ." without specifically citing the

Whether the "utter depoliticization" of the party would be a sign of its "strengthening" remains unclear.

In setting forth his own, quite different views on the reforms, Cleary argues that

> The splitting of the party into two separate hierarchies . . . is not in itself proof that more direct participation of the party in the management of the economy was intended. . . . [W]hat the reorganization has done is to establish definite lines of responsibility within the intermediate strata of the party hierarchy. . . . [T]he division of party organizations according to the "production principle" may be regarded as the logical outcome of the growing professional specialization of individual party members.[22]

On the whole, Cleary concludes that what was involved was a "relatively minor structural reform." Whether or not depoliticization of the party was intended by Khrushchev, it is obvious that Cleary's explanations of Khrushchev's intentions, as well as the interpretations of the experts whose opinions he disputes, were themselves "utterly depoliticized."

But Cleary and the subjects of his survey were writing *before* the fall of Khrushchev—that is, before they knew that the undoing of his reforms had become the first order of the day for his successors. They considered Khrushchev's attempt to reorganize the party not a "minor structural reform" but rather as highly political and explosive. According to *Pravda* (11/17/64), one month after Khrushchev was removed, the party was reunited and the rural district committees restored. Indeed, writing in 1972, Werner G. Hahn observed that

> these reorganizations kept the party in turmoil from top to bottom throughout 1962. The political frustration and unhappiness they caused undercut Khrushchev's support and became one of the prime reasons for his being removed from power. The opposition by local party officials suffering in the confusion, or even losing their positions, [was] reflected in the post-Khrushchev reversal of

observers who are the source of the "general consensus" or provide the "measure of agreement." In this situation I have relied heavily on Cleary's analysis and judgment.

[22]*Ibid.*, p. 60.

the bifurcation of party organs and the restoration of the *raikoms* [district committees].[23]

Jerry Hough, on the other hand, wrote his article "A Harebrained Scheme in Retrospect" after the political nature of the 1961-1962 reforms was clearly revealed. Nevertheless, he not only did not dispute the conclusion that only a "minor structural reform" was involved, but also advanced his own view that the reforms should be explained more in psychological than in political terms. According to Hough, Khrushchev was a "tinkering reformer—the man who, as defined by [Walter] Lippmann, is forever trying to make the existing machinery of government function perfectly in terms of some abstract ideal." These terms, says Hough, "surely provide the best explanation of the reasons that the [bifurcation] decision was recently reversed."[24] While cautioning that we should not "simply dismiss the 1962-1964 experiments as a nonsensical result produced by the impact of advancing age upon a mind which was already too fascinated with organizational changes," Hough insists that "the new Soviet leaders were correct in calling the bifurcation of the party organization a harebrained scheme."[25] The journal *Partiinaia zhizn'* [Party life], in its editorial of December 1964, explained the matter in approximately the same spirit, although less colorfully and without reference to Walter Lippmann.[26]

In any event, in all the cases cited above, the expert interpretations—both Western and Soviet—have not gone beyond purely administrative considerations. None has suggested that the outcome of the political crisis of 1960-1964 might have determined whether or not Russia was to take the "Hungarian" path, complete with comprehensive economic reform and general liberalization of the regime.[27]

---

[23]*The Politics of Soviet Agriculture* (Baltimore: Johns Hopkins University Press, 1972), p. 85.

[24]*Problems of Communism*, July-August 1965, p. 26.

[25]*Ibid.*, p. 29.

[26]1964, no. 23, p. 5.

[27]Perhaps Carl Linden, in his essay "Khrushchev and the Party Battle," came the closest to suggesting such a conclusion, especially in his penetrating observations that Khrushchev's approach "tends in effect toward the conversion of the party officialdom into a technocratic-managerial class conducting the mundane affairs of an advanced industrial society" and that "Khrushchev's reform could

THE END OF A PARTY AFFAIR

But was it purely coincidental that the reforms we are talking about followed directly after the Soviet Watergate and Khrushchev's attack on the "people with a hunger for metal?" Were not all these events the successive stages of a gradually developing political crisis? Let us see.

At the March Plenum of 1962, Khrushchev unexpectedly charged that Soviet agriculture was in effect not being managed by anyone. If we remember the old Stalinist view that culture and agriculture are party affairs, it is clear that Khrushchev's assertion verged on dangerous heresy. Just as before 1957 (and after 1964), it did not—for decades—enter anyone's head to question the belief that Soviet industry could only be properly administered by ministries located in the capital—that is, by the Central Economic Administration—so no one had ever doubted that the Soviet countryside could best be administered by the raikoms. We have assumed that Khrushchev needed the destruction of the ministries in 1957 not so much because of administrative as because of political considerations: the bureaucrats in the Central Economic Administration were the political constituency of the post-dictatorial oligarchy he sought to destroy. But if this is so, then what considerations led Khrushchev when he set about destroying the rural party committees by declaring that "by themselves the possibilities [inherent in collective economy] will yield nothing if we do not learn to manage agriculture?" He continued:

I would like to emphasize that I am not talking about general leadership, but specifically about the management of agricultural production. There are already more than enough institutions which give general leadership, and yet we do not have an agency . . . which can manage. Actually, we have not had such an agency during all the years of Soviet power.[28]

This was a slap in the face for those who for decades had thought of themselves as the only possible managers of Soviet agriculture.

only undercut the top- and middle-echelon party apparatchiki whose careers were in the sphere of political ideological work" (i.e., the "priests" in my terms) (*Problems of Communism*, September-October 1963, pp. 35, 32).

[28]Khrushchev, vol. 6, p. 398.

Khrushchev followed this with a devastating critique of their practices, which was not unlike Ovechkin's observations and my own (following the collective farmer with a club, reminding him that silage is not cured in barrels like sauerkraut, etc.). It was quite astonishing to hear such Novymirist language from a head of government—the more so since his critique would have done credit to Ovechkin himself. Recalling that according to its bylaws the kolkhoz "is a quite autonomous cooperative organization," Khrushchev asked:

> And what is the real state of affairs? In fact, we intervene in the life of the cooperative, until recently deciding even what crops, and how much of each, the kolkhoz should grow. . . . Now we decide what products and how much of each the cooperatives should sell. . . . The local organs even intervene in such trivial aspects of the life of the cooperative as deciding who should belong to the governing board and who should be nominated as chairman. The party organizations frequently send kolkhoz chairmen out from the cities.[29]

The astonished audience for this speech knew quite well that Khrushchev himself had initiated the sending of chairmen out from the cities. And no one until then (except the critics from *Novyi mir*) had seen anything at all wrong in the intervention of party professionals in the trivial affairs of the kolkhozy. This seemed to be part of the natural order of things, which is why such vehement attacks sounded especially strange on the lips of the leader of the party. There could be no doubt that in front of the whole nation he was betraying his former allies. The immediate question was: Who will gain from this coup d'etat? The answer became clear from Khrushchev's recommendation that district production directorates be set up which would become the institutions to manage the agriculture, as distinct from the general leadership provided by the little Stalins. For if management were now to pass into the hands of professional managers (as distinct from party professionals), what would remain for the district committees? General leadership? It would mean the end of agriculture as a party affair.

A short time afterward, in June 1962, at a meeting of staff members of the production directorates, Khrushchev explained (amid

[29]*Ibid.*, p. 403.

the audience's laughter) that he knew precisely the effects of this change: "The secretaries of the district committees of the party may ask: If the district committees are not to intervene in the solution of problems having to do with production, then what are they to do? This is a correct and legitimate question."[30] However, Khrushchev had no answer to that question—presumably because there wasn't one.

The little Stalins at the district level sounded the alarm as early as March 1962. Already they had perceived the political meaning of Khrushchev's recommendation, and they signaled their anxiety in a letter to the leader of the party. Khrushchev read their letter to the Plenum:

> The Central Committee of the party has received a letter. It is, to be sure, not signed, but the authors of the letter refer to themselves as secretaries of district committees of the party in Krasnodar and Stavropol' territories. The secretaries of the district committees, addressing me, write approximately as follows: "You have been a secretary of a district committee yourself. We are addressing you as our colleague, who knows the needs of the districts. Understand us and hear our voice—our SOS."[31]

Thus in sharp contrast to the experts referred to above, the rural party professionals had perceived the meaning of Khrushchev's proposal immediately. And they were crying "wolf." What they saw ahead was by no means a "minor structural reform." It was for them rather a harbinger of political catastrophe. And their fears were justified. Six months later the death sentence was pronounced on the rural district committees. "The local party organs," Khrushchev said at the November Plenum, "have determined that it is no longer desirable to have rural district committees in the party."[32]

What had happened, in effect, was that in March 1962 the National Leadership decided to permit open conflict in the countryside between the party professionals and the managerial elite. During six months of furious struggle, what remained of the party affair revealed something dumbfounding. It was simply not needed, and therefore it

[30] *Ibid.*, vol. 7, p. 60.
[31] *Ibid.*, vol. 6, p. 450.
[32] *Ibid.*, vol. 7, p. 327.

collapsed. Ovechkin's managers had beaten Kochetov's party professionals.

This was one of the most extraordinary reforms I ever observed in the USSR—in a sense, a minor revolution. Probably only people who have worked in the Soviet countryside can accurately gauge its significance. The party professionals were not driven out of the districts. They were simply transformed from dictators into secretaries of party committees of the production directorates—that is, they became counselors to the managers.

Nothing tragic happened to them—nothing, that is, apart from their being removed from power, and the transfer of this power into the hands of their bitter enemies. The professional managers—energetic, enterprising, and self-confident, who had come out of the universities, the editorial offices, and the kolkhozy, and who, as we know from the diatribes of Ovechkin's heroes (having seen his Martynov, we have seen them all), could not stand the little Stalins—now unmercifully baited the former dictators of the districts as ignorant and incompetent people, indeed as a hindrance.

Khrushchev could endeavor to console these suffering party professionals with the notion that they were equal in status to the heads of the production directorates—that they were "like two brothers, both elder to an equal degree."[33] And Hough can cite Smirnitsky's dictionary to support this consoling assertion.[34] But I saw this dramatic role reversal with my own eyes, and I bear witness that nothing of the kind was conceivable under Soviet rule before or after Khrushchev. The former Olympians who just yesterday had raised people up and cast them down into the abyss of oblivion, who had held in their hands all the threads of life, now lay around under foot, needed by no one, confused, impotent—having lost, it seems, not only status and power, but their very role in life. The official journal *Partiinaia zhizn'*, usually as dull as an autumn rain, suddenly found its tongue, exposing these fallen gods in sarcastic language:

> The practice of economic leadership which was widespread at one time, and which suffered from overblown rhetoric and a superficial approach to the problems of production, gave rise in some people

[33]*Ibid.*, p. 446.
[34]*Problems of Communism*, July-August 1965, p. 31.

to the incorrect notion that political leadership of the economy was nothing other than leadership "in general and on the whole"—leadership by means of appeals and slogans.[35]

For most of their lives these people had been party professionals, exercising leadership "in general and on the whole." They did not know how to do anything else. Even if they were educated, they had long since lost their qualifications. What they knew how to do was no longer needed, and what was necessary they did not know how to do. This was the drama of a whole class of people who before our eyes were transformed from the lords of life into a kind of *lumpens*, into spongers and "superfluous people."

Of course, this did not happen immediately everywhere. In certain districts which did not have strong managerial leaders (their Martynovs), the party professionals continued to grasp desperately at power and play their old games. Khrushchev himself commented on this, using the example of the Orel production directorate. He condemned their behavior, saying that such "people have party cards, but do not have a correct understanding of party leadership."[36] The managers, however, needed no protection from on high. As soon as conditions for free competition with the party professionals existed, they appeared perfectly capable of handling it by themselves. Like the leaders of the Link Reform, such as Pervitskii, who victoriously competed with a kolkhoz brigade, they needed only one thing—that no one interfere in their struggle with the little Stalins. In a fair competition—one on one—they beat their opponents easily.

The metamorphosis of the former Olympians into "superfluous people" was one of the most vivid impressions of my life as a journalist, and to a significant degree determined the subsequent development of my views. Before my eyes there emerged, in essence, a demonstration of how the Soviet countryside would have looked without the Soviet prefects, if the reform process had not been blocked.

I was personally acquainted with some of the people who participated in this reform. They included, for example, Aleksandr Erkaev from the Kuban' and Iosif Shtarberg from the Amur. They were

[35]1963, no. 2, p. 19.
[36]Khrushchev, vol. 7, p. 446.

not only competent specialists and rational thinkers, but they were bursting with ideas. The manuscript of a recent history of the Stalin collectivization (the so-called Danilov manuscript), which had been prepared for the press by the Institute of History of the Academy of Sciences (but has never been published), passed from hand to hand among the new managers—one of the first swallows of the *samizdat*, when no samizdat was supposed to exist.[37] At that time I traveled around the country a great deal, and there was no rural district where I did not see that sheaf of papers, like a Bible, on the desks of heads of production directorates. Among other things, this manuscript was the first serious scholarly attempt to revise the official postulates by which the Soviet countryside was ruled since the end of the 1920s. Danilov's study was, as it were, a historical validation of the ideas of the new rural managers, who were actively seeking an alternative approach, just as they were seeking a social base, a constituency. They found both in the new peasant elite and in the mass movement which was beginning in its midst.

The country awakened from a quarter-century of lethargy. The new managerial elite, which had just emerged into the light, grasped at the Link Reform because, for the first time, after two generations of silence during which all social initiatives were monopolized first by Stalin and then by his heirs, the Soviet prefects, the opportunity to think and act had opened up. Intellectuals and their ideas were again needed by the fatherland, which seemed to have forgotten about them. And this was true primarily of the most vulnerable part of the system, its Achilles heel—agriculture.

This miracle could happen, however, only because the years 1960-1964 were marked by the emergence of these link and managerial rural elites. As noted in the preceding chapter, the key question was: Why were these new elites allowed to emerge in Soviet society at this time? The only explanation I can think of involves the swiftly developing establishment crisis. Trying to survive under the repeated blows of Khrushchev's merciless hammer, the Soviet prefects were unable to prevent the developing alliance between the new managers and the peasant elite, the result of which was the first wave of the Link Reform. It was in this sense that the abolition of the rural party

[37]For more detail on Danilov and his project, see A. Nekrich, *Otreshis' ot strakha* [Renounce fear] (London, 1979), p. 251.

district committees in 1962 can be seen as the logical continuation of the Soviet Watergate—the purge of the corrupt party professionals in 1960-1961. In 1962 Khrushchev went beyond Ovechkin's remedy.

DEAD CELLS

Even before the fateful reorganization, however, Khrushchev tried to do something more: he conceived a plan for making the purge of the little Stalins permanent by means of a change in the party by-laws. The most significant thing about these new bylaws was an article limiting the tenure of party professionals in their posts. The practical effect of this would be the alteration of the makeup of the Plenum of the Central Committee at each election by at least one-fourth, and the makeup of the party and state leadership of the republics and provinces by at least one-third.[38]

In practice this change of personnel meant that over the course of a single decade the corps of the party professionals now in power in the provincial and district committees would be replaced in its entirety. Only a few of the little Stalins who occupied their positions in 1961, say, would still retain them in 1970. The same applied to the state leaders: they were automatically expelled from the game. The only elite not subject to this implacable process was the managerial elite.

Perhaps most remarkable of all, however, was *how* Khrushchev defended this change in the bylaws:

> Whereas in the first years of the revolution, the circle of Communist leaders was a narrow one, at present the opportunities for promoting new people to leading posts are inexhaustible. We must set up an order of things whereby the comrades elected to leading posts do not block the road for new forces. . . . Should we remain within the circle of one and the same people who once were elected to leading organs? This is not our course.[39]

Only nine months had passed from the time when, relying on an analogous argument (the de-Stalinization formula), Khrushchev had

[38]F. R. Kozlov, "Ob izmeneniakh v Ustave KPSS" [On changes in the bylaws of the CPSU], in *XXII S'ezd* . . . , vol. 3, p. 13.

[39]*Ibid.*, vol. 1, p. 252.

challenged the "comrades [who] have developed a hunger for metal."
Once again, he divided Soviet history into two fundamentally distinct
periods. In the first (Stalinist) period, resources—both material and
human—were scarce, and it was necessary to concentrate on heavy
industry and defense, and to confine leadership to the narrow circle
of leading Communist personnel. Now that period of Soviet history
has passed. There is an abundance of human and material resources,
and it is time to select new leaders. Khrushchev continued:

> It is no secret that there are among us comrades who at one
> time were . . . elected to leading posts and who have continued to
> occupy them for whole decades. During this time some of them
> have lost the capacity to do business in a creative way, have lost
> the feeling of the new, have become a hindrance. To leave such
> people in their posts longer merely because they were at one time
> elected would be incorrect. . . . Every organism is made up of indi-
> vidual cells, and is constantly renewed because while some cells
> die, new ones are born. . . . We cannot stop or interrupt this natural
> process.[40]

The reader can imagine with what horror the "comrades . . . elected
to leading posts" heard, 20 years ago, the heretical reasoning of their
leader by glancing at the present makeup of the Politburo, where the
average age of the "dead cells" is about 70, and where the comrades
intend to sit at their posts until they die.

Thus, during the course of 1961, Khrushchev clearly identified
all the political opponents of the process of reform—that is, the establishment groups which did not share his (and Malenkov's) formula
of de-Stalinization. And when to the list of people with a hunger for
metal (the military-industrial complex) and hidebound dogmatists
(the professional ideologues), we add the dead cells who had been
elected to leading posts (the little Stalins), we have the same people
who had brought Khrushchev to power in the Kremlin revolt of 1957.

THE PREFECTS VS. THE PREFECTS

In such a political context, the division of the provincial hierarchy into industrial and rural committees (which was, ironically,

[40]*Ibid.*, pp. 253-54.

announced at the same Plenum of November 1962 at which the rural district committees were liquidated) must have seemed very different from a "harebrained scheme." However, to go to the opposite extreme—as did certain spokesmen of the Link Reform in Moscow and quite a few party professionals in the provinces—of interpreting this split as the introduction of a two-party system in the USSR is hardly justified. As one of the leading Soviet experts on party organization said:

> There is no basis for the fears expressed by some comrades that the division of party organizations and Soviets . . . will destroy the normal relationships between city and countryside. . . . The division by no means signifies that the entire party is being divided or that we will now have two parties—one in the city and the other in the countryside.[41]

It cannot be denied, however, that the division of the provincial committees led immediately to heated confrontations. The prefects who headed the rural provincial committees, and who now became fully responsible for the functioning of agriculture, suddenly had their eyes opened. It was as if only at this moment did they understand the practical effects of the Stalinist "general line"—i.e., a catastrophic shortage in the countryside of almost everything that was needed—trucks, equipment, roads, building materials, fertilizer, and, most important, money. Only now, a decade later, did they grasp the real significance of the de-Stalinization formula. Over the course of a quarter century the countryside had been the stepchild of the state—underfed, underclothed, neglected, humiliated. And so powerful was the inertia of the Stalinist policies that even the sanctimonious speeches of the leaders and state plans couldn't do much to break it. It was suddenly discovered, for example, that, for some unknown reason, 13 billion rubles allocated by the Seven-Year Plan to agricultural equipment and irrigation had disappeared. Although the number of sovkhozy had greatly increased between 1956 and 1961, the capital investment in sovkhoz production in 1961 remained at the 1956 level. As a result, their losses increased by 3 billion rubles.[42] The supply of mineral fertilizer to the countryside had not increased

[41]F. Petrenko, in *Partiinaia zhizn'*, no. 2, 1963, p. 18.

[42]Khrushchev, vol. 4, p. 181.

between 1958 and 1960. In 1957 the plants which were not part of the system of agricultural machine-building supplied the countryside with machines to the value of 370 million rubles; in 1961 they supplied only 90 million rubles' worth. The number of tractors sold to the countryside fell instead of increasing (as had been planned) from 258,000 in 1957 to 236,000 in 1959, while the production of combines—both for harvesting and silage—dropped, respectively, by a factor of 2.5 and a factor of 4.[43] In short, the situation was disastrous, and was likely to get even worse: the plan for 1962 allocated 30.5 billion rubles for capital investment in industry but only 7.6 billion for investment in agriculture.[44]

Under these conditions, is it surprising that the confrontations which arose between the prefects of the city and those of the countryside were often intensely hostile? The rural prefects suspected that their urban counterparts were intriguing against the countryside, depriving them of goods that were in short supply, and using their connections in the military and in the State Planning Agency, the State Bank, and the Ministry of Finance to alter on the sly plans for allocation of resources which had already been approved. They felt themselves outflanked and outsmarted; they were smothered in indignation. One could see them scurrying along the corridors of the State Planning Agency or between the departments of the Central Committee, where they showed their rage, fought, beat their fists on the tables, complained that the impossible was being asked of them, fired off statistics in machine-gun volleys—and incessantly made demands in the name of the countryside, in the name of justice, in the name of daily bread. Meanwhile their opponents, the urban prefects, piously intoned the general line and party traditions, and accused the rural prefects of "capitulationism."

Suddenly—almost overnight, it seemed—the provincial caucus in the "parliament" was split. It was now unthinkable that the rural prefects could vote as one with the urban prefects—on any question whatever. There was one exception, of course—i.e., the liquidation of the "harebrained scheme" which had split the provincial committees and had so unexpectedly put them in the unnatural position of sworn enemies of the Stalinist general line and partisans of the

[43]*Ibid.*, pp. 252-53.

[44]*Voprosy ekonomiki*, no. 1, 1963, p. 71.

de-Stalinization formula. A strong case could be made that if such a state of affairs had lasted for even three years (until the following congress of the party, scheduled for 1965), a fundamentally new arrangement of forces both in the "parliament" and in the Soviet establishment as a whole could have emerged. To be more precise, a new "parliamentary" coalition could have been formed, with perhaps a strong bloc combining the rural prefects with the new managerial elite of the countryside and the peasant elite of the links against the "steel-eaters," including the military-industrial complex and the urban prefects. This might have been a genuine breakthrough.

THE VISION OF THE FUTURE

History generally has little sympathy for lost causes. That which does not succeed it is inclined to treat as something misguided—if not harebrained. In retrospect, it is difficult now even to imagine the agitated atmosphere of the establishment crisis period, saturated as it was with the most fantastic expectations and electrically charged with high hopes.

What was the reformist party so excited about? What so inspired the managers? Was it indeed only "minor structural reforms?" Even the passionate anti-Stalinist speeches from the podium of the 22nd party congress, even the publication of Solzhenitsyn's "One Day in the Life of Ivan Denisovich" in *Novyi mir* and Yevtushenko's poem "Stalin's Heirs" in *Pravda* cannot fully explain the excitement and the hopes which suddenly swept across the country. Not just a change, but The Change is coming—such seemed to be the general feeling. Something fundamental was in the making. The old, rusty Stalinist system—our shame and disgrace—was at last disintegrating beyond repair. Such was the dream many of us lived with in the short but dramatic reformist interval between terror and stagnation that reached its climax in 1960-1964. Some may consider it childish enthusiasm. I would call it the "spirit of Reform."

There had to be some meaning to all the devastating blows rained down on the heads of Khrushchev's former allies and our enemies. It couldn't be all for naught that the Stalinist general line, the iron law of the party, was so thoroughly compromised—until Khrushchev finally declared it inoperative. The Soviet Watergate had indeed decimated the ranks of the party professionals of Stalin's generation, and the new party bylaws had written their permanent replacement into law. Was it conceivable that all these things were mere coincidence—the Link Reform, the emergence of a new rural elite, the triumph of the rural managers resulting in the abolition of the district party committees, the retreat of the military, the division of Soviet prefects into two hierarchies confronting each other, making all but impossible their traditional dominance? And then there was public discussion of comprehensive economic reform to boot, including demands for managerial autonomy in industry and the rehabilitation of the "heretical" concept of profit.

To many of us it looked like more than coincidence. To us it looked like a vision of a future worth working for. Who knows if the realization of our vision was possible? The hopes were there, and the reforms needed for their realization seemed to be there too. Hundreds of thousands of people were involved in them. For all these people, the vision was a reality—not mere fantasy.

Imagine for a moment that Khrushchev had survived the crisis of 1964, as he had managed to survive many previous crises, and that the reforms which were already in place had continued their development. What could have happened in the course of a single decade, say? Would it not have been a continuing repetition of what had already happened in the Soviet countryside in 1962-1964? Open conflict between the party professionals and the managerial elite would have resulted in the defeat (or at least a retreat) of the former. Even more would this have been so in the 1970s if the new bylaws, which had thrown down the gauntlet not only to party professionals but also, it seems, to party professionalism itself, had remained in force. Then, if this analysis is correct, a stable and competent middle managerial class would be confronting a shifting, destabilized, and demoralized crowd of party amateurs, who would have suffered the same fate of becoming "superfluous people" which had already overtaken the former bosses of the rural districts.

Our Russian destiny determined otherwise. To a great degree it was the fault of the National Leadership. The reformers were not introduced into the "parliament," which remained dominated by the provincial elites. A well-conceived political strategy was lacking. The party professionals were not sufficiently demoralized to make their reunion impossible. In October 1964 the urban and rural prefects united on the sole question on which they were still capable of uniting, and the major reforms were terminated. The reformist leader proved incapable of consolidating his allies politically and of making permanent the changes resulting from his reforms. Like all the Russian reformers who had preceded him, Khrushchev failed to make the Reform irreversible.

It is possible to ask why the breakthrough in the Reform which Kadar succeeded in making in the 1970s eluded Khrushchev a decade earlier. And it is possible to ask if the melancholy finale of the Soviet 1960s could have been prevented, and if so, under what conditions. But what strikes me as impossible is to dismiss this profound political drama as a "minor structural reform" or a "harebrained scheme."

ISOLATION OF THE REFORMIST LEADER

I don't know if the melancholy finale of this drama could have been changed by anything Western intellectuals said or did. It is a fact, however, that Khrushchev had to fight a struggle on two fronts— against his own *and* the Western military-industrial complexes. A recent interview with former Secretary of Defense Robert McNamara is very revealing on this point:

> [I] f I had been the Soviet secretary of defense, I'd have been worried as hell about the imbalance of forces. And I would have been concerned that the United States was trying to build a first-strike capability. . . . I would have heard the rumors that the Air Force was recommending achievement of such a capability. You put those two things together: a known force disadvantage that is large enough in itself to at least appear to support the view that the United States was planning a first-strike capability and, secondly, talk about U.S. personnel that that was the objective—it would have just scared the hell out of me.[45]

It would have scared the hell out of Khrushchev too—precisely at the point when he was trying desperately to bridle his own military. If Kochetov, for example, could have invented something really effective

[45]Quoted in Robert Scheer, *With Enough Shovels* (New York: Random House, 1982), p. 217.

to undermine Khrushchev's case against the "steel-eaters," it would have been precisely the kind of thing McNamara was describing. It is unlikely that those in the United States who were pushing for the achievement of a first-strike capability at the time of the establishment crisis in Moscow were seeking to secure the triumph of the "steel-eaters." Most probably they didn't care: for them Stalin, king of the "steel-eaters," and Khrushchev, their sworn enemy, must have seemed like totalitarian twin brothers. But did American intellectuals consider that the triumph of the "steel-eaters" over Khrushchev would almost inevitably result in a relentless arms race in the decades ahead? Even in the role of Kremlin-watchers, Western intellectuals might have been helpful in alerting Khrushchev and the people around him to ominous signs which were extremely difficult if not impossible to discern from within. For example, a sensitive observer, in October 1961 say, at the zenith of Khrushchev's power, might have discerned behind the official enthusiasm and oaths of undying love to the "faithful Leninist" and the "great son of the Soviet people," the unmistakable signs that clouds were gathering over the leader's head. It would have sufficed to read *Oktiabr'* attentively, and in particular the novels of Kochetov. And there were other ominous signs of the growing isolation of the leader.

We have already noted that the ideological context for all of Khrushchev's reforms was the de-Stalinization formula and the struggle against the cult of personality (i.e., dictatorship) which followed naturally from it. It is not so widely known that Khrushchev grounded the reform with the most fatal consequences for the party professionals—the change in the party bylaws—on the need to make de-Stalinization *irreversible*. Consider what he said at the 22nd party congress:

> Constant renewal of the personnel . . . is based, in particular, on the lessons to be learned from the consequences of the cult of the personality of I. V. Stalin. I've already had occasion to speak of this more than once. . . . In the draft program and bylaws—those two major documents of the party—positions are formulated which should create a guarantee against recurrences of the cult of personality and erect a solid barrier in its path. From the podium of the Congress we declare: the party must take all necessary steps so that the path of the cult of personality is closed forever.[46]

[46]*XXII S'ezd* . . . , vol. 1, p. 253.

This was a declaration of basic importance; after all, "closing forever" the path to the restoration of the dictatorship has been at the root of every major Russian Reform. (It is worthy of note that the words "we declare," as used by Khrushchev, were completely out of place in the context of a party congress—unless we suspect Khrushchev of intentionally expressing himself, like the Russian emperors, in the first-person plural.)

The report on the changes in the bylaws was made by Frol Kozlov, the former prefect of Leningrad, who had had a dizzying career, reaching the position of number two man in the party. More than three-fourths of those who spoke on Kozlov's report were party professionals—first and second secretaries of provincial and republican committees—plus their literary representative, Kochetov, editor of *Oktiabr'*, who was known by everyone to be Kozlov's man. Not one of these speakers referred in any way to the need for a "constant renewal of personnel" as a guarantee against the restoration of Stalinism, or as Khrushchev expressed it, to "erect a solid barrier in its path." Kozlov almost openly refused to discuss this "barrier," referring instead to the fact that "in the report of Nikita Sergeevich Khrushchev on the program of the CPSU, the need to introduce new personnel in important positions is profoundly and comprehensively validated."[47] For Kozlov, the essence of the bylaws lay in something quite different—namely, that they "provide for a broad influx of new, fresh forces into the party agencies of the country, and for a correct combination of old and young personnel."[48] He acknowledged that "the process of renewal of the leading personnel must become the norm of party life. For this reason, this process is provided for in the program and the bylaws of the party and is made one of the laws of party life."[49] But at the same point he noted, as if reassuring his audience (and perhaps his own little Stalin soul), that the "process of renewal" had already taken place prior to the congress in 1960-1961, at the time of the Soviet Watergate, when 45 percent of the members of the Central Committees of the republics, as well as the territorial and provincial committees, had been replaced with new people. This made it sound as though the "correct combination of old and young

[47]*Ibid.*, vol. 3, p. 13.
[48]*Ibid.*
[49]*Ibid.*, p. 14.

personnel" had already been achieved and that he was now addressing the "new, fresh forces" whose influx into the leadership the new by-laws provided for. Thus, for the immediate future, these people who now filled the Hall of the Palace of Soviets had nothing to worry about. This was particularly true since

> the principle of systematic renewal of the party agencies is closely connected with the principle of continuity of leadership. It by no means negates the important role of experienced, authoritative officeholders. Without a more or less stable group of leaders, continuity of leadership cannot be provided. . . . For this reason it is said in the draft of the bylaws that specific party figures or officeholders in the party can, in view of their recognized authority and high political and organizing qualities, be elected to leading agencies for a longer period of time.[50]

In a further effort to soften the blow, Kozlov allowed himself a rather free interpretation of the program. The program said:

> A higher phase in the development of the party itself, its political, ideological, and organizational work, corresponds to the full-scale construction of Communism. The party will without interruption improve the forms and methods of its work so that the level of its leadership . . . corresponds to the increasing demands of the epoch of the building of Communism.[51]

Kozlov interpreted this passage in this way:

> The bylaws of the CPSU, which our congress is adopting, . . . raise still higher the party's role as the inspirer and organizer of the building of Communism. [The bylaws constitute] the validation of the increased role [of the party] in the life of society during the period of full-scale construction of Communism.[52]

As we can see, the program speaks of raising the *level of leadership* of the party, while Kozlov emphasizes increasing the *role* of the party. At first glance it may seem that there is no contradiction here, since raising the level of leadership may involve increasing the role.

[50]*Ibid.*, p. 15.
[51]*Ibid.*
[52]*Ibid.*, pp. 6, 5.

What is at issue is the nuance, the difference in emphasis, which, as we will see, the little Stalins immediately caught in Kozlov's report, and to which they responded with enthusiasm.

Of the fourteen little Stalins who spoke, twelve did not comment at all on the central thesis of the new party constitution. They preferred to speak on other subjects—the crimes of the "anti-party group" (that is, the disgraced oligarchs), the overfulfillment of the plan in their provinces, the need to remove Stalin's body from the mausoleum, the yield of steel and fish, and even the heresy of the Albanian Communists—in a word, anything except the point at issue for the discussion of which they had formally ascended the dais of the congress. The two who did speak on the substance of the issue did so in the following manner:

[T]he party bylaws contain an article to the effect that particular party figures and officeholders, because of their recognized authority, may be elected for longer periods of time. This provision of the bylaws proceeds from what Lenin said about the role and authority of leaders. Having taken all steps to exclude the possibility of manifestations of the cult of personality, the party *has safeguarded and will safeguard in the future the authority of party figures* who have dedicated themselves to the service of the people—an authority which is recognized by communists and all the people. For this reason, this provision, which has tremendous significance and profound meaning, was unanimously supported during the discussion of the bylaws by all communists.[53]

As we can see, following Kozlov's lead, the speaker interprets the bylaws not so much as a safeguard against the restoration of the dictatorship, as Khrushchev had intended, but rather as a safeguard for the preservation of party professionalism.

The general views of the little Stalins were summed up by S. M. Shchetinin, the first secretary of the Irkutsk provincial committee. Fully embracing Kozlov's formulation he totally ignored Khrushchev's: "The primary significance of the draft bylaws lies in the fact that they . . . raise still higher the role of the party as the inspirer and

[53]*Ibid.*, pp. 80-81. This is from the speech of O. P. Kolchina, Secretary of Moscow Provincial Committee. (Emphasis added.)

organizer of the struggle of the Soviet people for the victory of Communism."[54]

Thus, all the speakers on the new bylaws tried to distance themselves from the tendencies destructive of party professionalism. Even Kozlov and the two little Stalins who were willing to speak on the substance of Khrushchev's pronouncement about "constant renewal" (which differentiated the new party constitution from the previous ones) did so in order to emphasize "continuity" (which linked the new with the old). Khrushchev proved to be the only speaker at the congress for whom preventing the restoration of the dictatorship appeared to be essential. To the accompaniment of droning, monotonous recitals in praise of the "great Leninist," the party professionals decisively refused to follow their leader in this crucial dimension of the Reform—as early as October 1961.

And these were his own people, his clients who replaced the "bankrupt" and unfaithful allies of 1957. The logical question for Khrushchev to ask himself at this point was: Would these clients who betrayed him now at the zenith of his power stay with him when his hour of need came? Would they break into the Kremlin in a desperate attempt to save him from *new* conspirators as their predecessors had done in June 1957? Could he still rely on the "patron-client" relationship if his reformist drive so obviously opposed these clients' group interests? And if they were likely to betray him in case of a new showdown in the National Leadership, shouldn't some safeguards against them be erected immediately, instead of waiting until the next congress in 1965? Shouldn't "new, fresh forces" be introduced into the "parliament" right away so they could defend him if the opponents struck? And shouldn't these new people be chosen from among those whose group interests coincide with his own in order for him to have in them not only clients but also collaborators who share his views?

He still had time to do this, as we know now, if he had listened less to his clients' ritual exercises and more to the content of their messages. There were at least three years to go. And yet he, the crafty manipulator, appeared to be as overwhelmed by political inertia as the "weakling" Alexander Dubček was, seven years after that in Prague, when faced with the threat of Soviet invasion. Both hadn't even begun

[54]*Ibid.*, p. 171.

to realize the treacherous and merciless character of the anti-reformist forces they were facing. Both failed to recognize their growing political isolation. Neither was prepared for a showdown. Both were beaten by their former allies. Both paid for their lack of political insight not only with their own political death, but also with the crushing defeat of the cause they represented.

WAS THE OCTOBER 1964 COUP INEVITABLE?

However convincing all these explanations may sound, were they indeed decisive for the success of the coup that eliminated Khrushchev from the Russian political scene—and with him the reformist regime? In other words, was the coup inevitable, or it could have been averted by, say, a series of major successes in the international arena which could have given Khrushchev more time to consolidate and perhaps institutionalize the reformist constituencies by creating, for example, a powerful "parliamentary caucus" ready to defend him in case of a new showdown in the National Leadership?

It might be supposed that he was halfway to such a solution. Alone among Soviet leaders before and after him, he invited both rural and urban managers and academics, along with members of the reborn peasant elite (sometimes in large numbers), to participate in "parliamentary" sessions. The next essential step would be to break the old Stalinist electoral system, which is the principal basis for the domination by party professionals of the Soviet parliamentary scene, and give the necessary voting power to the new elites. In a sense such a solution was implicit in the new party constitution adopted in 1961.

If this analysis is correct, then what Khrushchev needed most in this critical period of transition from one power base to another was not miracles or a return to the good graces of his former allies, but simply *time*. He needed time to complete his major program of removing the party professionals as directors of Soviet agriculture and replacing them with rural managers and the peasant elite. He needed time to introduce the managerial autonomy in industry about which debate had been raging in the Soviet press since 1962. In short, Khrushchev needed time to accomplish within Soviet society what Kadar accomplished in Hungary. Above all, he needed time to curb the military and halt the arms race on the basis of a military doctrine very similar to that being advocated at the same time by Admiral Arleigh Burke of the U.S. Navy. Admiral Burke summarized this doctrine in the following terms:

> In making our retaliatory force secure from enemy attack, we do not need a great number of missiles and bombers. Whether the USSR has one half as many or several times as many missiles as the United States is really academic as long as we have the assured capability of destroying Russia and as long as the Soviets know it and are really convinced of it.[55]

This doctrine of "minimum deterrence" must have been shared by Khrushchev. Otherwise it would be impossible to explain how Khrushchev, when faced with the undeniable fact of American strategic superiority (which, according to Robert McNamara, should have "scared the hell" out of a Soviet Secretary of Defense) could have vehemently advocated the reduction of Soviet military expenditures as well as its conventional forces until his last day in office. There can be little doubt that if Admiral Burke's doctrine of minimum deterrence had prevailed in U.S. military planning circles at the time of the Soviet establishment crisis (thus giving Khrushchev sufficient grounds for defending a similar strategic policy against the Soviet military), the arms race of the 1970s could have been averted.[56]

---

[55]Quoted in George Lowe, *The Age of Deterrence* (Boston: Little, Brown, 1964), p. 197.

[56]George Breslauer quotes one of Khrushchev's statements to this effect: "The modernization of our army took years of work and cost billions. However, once we had equipped ourselves with the missiles, airplanes, submarine fleet, and nuclear warheads needed for our defense, we were able to reconsider our military budget." It is rather surprising that Breslauer adds the caustic comment "Unfortunately, Khrushchev's testimony does not reveal whether his decision to 'reconsider our military budget' came in 1961-1963 . . . or *still later*" (*Khrushchev and Brezhnev as Leaders* [London: George Allen and Unwin, 1982], p. 92; emphasis added), suggesting that Khrushchev could have thought it up in the quiet of his retirement. Such a suggestion seems especially strange since Breslauer knows that in April 1963 Khrushchev "delivered a hard-hitting speech . . . declaring that the Soviet economy could produce 'nothing but rockets.' At the December 1963 and February 1964 Plenums, he argued vehemently for massive

On the other hand, a coup like that of October 1964 must have been extremely hard to engineer, especially for those who had witnessed the political massacre in which the previous (June 1957) attempt at such a coup ended for the majority of the oligarchy. For such a coup to be successful, complete unanimity of the National Leadership was needed, which meant that in effect every single member could have exercised a veto. Not only could one dissenter have alerted Khrushchev, but a few might have formed a dissenting minority as in 1957, initiating a "parliamentary" battle with unpredictable results. This meant that men of compromise like Mikoyan or Brezhnev might have preferred to stay away from the enterprise — Mikoyan because he had little to win, Brezhnev because he had too much to lose as the heir apparent designated for leadership after Khrushchev. In that situation every member of the National Leadership must have been firmly convinced that Khrushchev is doomed, his appeal is ultimately lost, and he is unable to produce any success in either the domestic or international arena.

That might have been the case in 1964 for the domestic arena, where Khrushchev's opponents were strong enough to block his efforts. But they had little or no control over the international arena. Here was the Achilles' heel of the new conspirators. Here was a possible way to secure Khrushchev's survival. There was little hope for a fundamental proposal to reduce American strategic forces to the level of the Soviet forces in exchange for the reduction of Soviet conventional forces to the level of the American (which by accepting the principle of military parity between the superpowers could have ended the arms race), but there were less drastic means available to give the reformist leader a fighting chance in his hour of need. Even a hint of a "major international thaw" (to use Breslauer's phrase), on which Khrushchev's domestic program of 1963-1964 was predicated, might have sufficed, given the extreme uncertainty in the National Leadership. A solemn West German declaration that it would never join the nuclear club might have been enough. (Khrushchev himself

investments in the chemicals industry, paid for by cuts in the defense budget for 1964 [and] possible future troop reductions..." Breslauer also knows that by summer/fall 1964 "Khrushchev's investment priorities had ... become sufficiently reallocative that a major international thaw would facilitate the reduction in defense expenditures that the consumer program required" (*ibid.*, p. 96).

must have thought of this: wasn't it why he sent his son-in-law to Bonn on the eve of the coup?) A trip by President Kennedy to Moscow, similar to President Nixon's in 1972, would have been even better. (Khrushchev had invited Kennedy.) And best of all would have been a Western loan big enough to finance his major projects. In other words, in order to survive at the beginning of the 1960s, Khrushchev might have needed from the West nothing more than Brezhnev got so easily at the beginning of the next decade. There was a difference, however: Brezhnev, the leader of the regime of political stagnation, needed a major international thaw to strangle the reform and accelerate the military buildup while Khrushchev, the leader of the reformist regime, needed a thaw to deepen the reform and halt the arms race.

To be able to discern this difference and then to throw its weight behind the preservation of a reformist regime in the USSR, the West needed a much more subtle comprehension of how the post-totalitarian state works and a more acute intellectual insight into the real situation than it had. Its choice was not simply a matter of political feasibility of this or that action or of policy preferences, but was rooted in basic philosophical-historical assumptions about the nature of the post-totalitarian state and the patterns of change in the Russian political system. If the politicians of the West had any real insight into the workings of the Soviet system, they might have understood that the downfall of Khrushchev in the middle of an incomplete reformist attempt meant the end of an era. That as unpleasant as he might have been, his replacement would be much worse—not just for Russia but for the world as well. That as soon as Khrushchev was removed from office, an era of an infinitely dangerous nuclear arms race would descend on the world inexorably.

We all know that the necessary comprehension of the Soviet system was lacking in the West in 1964. But the hypothesis that the October coup could have been averted if the West had come to the rescue of a Russian reformist leader has implications for the future. Nikita Khrushchev was perhaps not the last reformist leader of Russia in the twentieth century, and a similar situation might develop in the 1980s or 1990s. It is essential that another opportunity of such historical magnitude not be lost. Is it possible that the West could lose such a chance again if it came? Let us look at the sovietological record.

In 1963 Thomas H. Rigby was seriously considering the analogy "between the post-1957 Khrushchev and the pre-1937 Stalin,"[57] while Robert Conquest conjectured that "If the best should come to the best, it might well be that the Khrushchev era would rank with other attempts to combine despotism with relaxation";[58] for Merle Fainsod in 1965 Khrushchev was "one of Stalin's lieutenants [who] had a pragmatic bent";[59] for Zbigniew Brzezinski, "By the time he was removed, Khrushchev had become an anachronism in the new political context he himself helped to create";[60] for Jerry Hough, as we know, Khrushchev was a "harebrained schemer." And even William Safire observes with splendid disdain that "Khrushchevian calls for decentralization have been heard before and such 'reform' has even been permitted in Hungary."[61] I have included Safire with the cohort of sovietologists quoted above because he puts the word *reform* in quotation marks, which seems to be a fairly accurate summary of all their views. He also directly associates Khrushchev with the Kadar reform which, whatever Safire may think of it, has provided Hungary not only with relative material well-being (unlike other provinces of the Soviet empire, it does not experience consumer goods shortages or food crises) but also with a liberal government— by authoritarian standards.

A Hungarian-type reform is perhaps what might have been expected from Khrushchev if he had been saved in the fateful days of October 1964—or from any "Russian Kadar" if he appears on the Soviet horizon. What the sovietologists cited above failed to see in Khrushchev was the genuine innovative potential of his reform. Their angle of vision prevented them from perceiving the significance of the Link Reform and, even more important, of the peasant elite reborn in that movement as a reformist constituency. Similarly they did not perceive that the rural managerial elite, fresh from their victory over the party professionals, were solidly behind Khrushchev.

[57]"The Extent and the Limits of Authority," *Problems of Communism*, September-October 1963, p. 38.

[58]"After Khrushchev: A Conservative Restoration," *ibid.*, p. 42.

[59]"Khrushchev in Retrospect," in *ibid.*, January-February 1965, pp. 2-3.

[60]"The Soviet Political System: Transformation or Degeneration?," *ibid.*, January-February 1966, p. 4.

[61]"Ninotchka and Tatyana," *New York Times*, 12/4/83.

They did not take much account of the hopes generated in the urban managerial class by the debate on managerial autonomy and by the new party "constitution," which undermined the very ethos of party professionalism. In short, a call to save Khrushchev would not have come from these quarters in 1964, and it is unlikely to come from there in any similar situation in the future. Even if we take the alternative view of Khrushchev as an "embattled consumer advocate," which Breslauer refers to as "conventional wisdom of the field among American political scientists," and which he challenges in his recent book on Khrushchev and Brezhnev,[62] there is still no explanation for the emergence of the broad reformist constituency during the establishment crisis as long as we continue to look at the post-totalitarian state "through an oligarchical perspective."[63]

Perhaps nowhere else is the basic difference between all these conventional approaches and the approach suggested in this study more apparent than in Breslauer's statement that the far-reaching anti-Stalinist campaign renewed in the course of the establishment crisis of 1960-1964 "led to, and encouraged, the public flowering of anti-Establishment poets, the publication of Alexander Solzhenitsyn's *One Day in the Life of Ivan Denisovich*, the coalescence of an anti-Establishment coterie around the journal *Novy Mir*, and a period of freedom in research and writing about party history unparalleled since the early 1930s."[64]

The head of an "anti-establishment coterie" is probably how people at the top of the Soviet scientific community viewed Andrey Sakharov when he deserted them in the late 1960s to become leader of the human rights movement. One cannot imagine, however, that after taking that step Sakharov might have been elected a member of the Central Committee of the CPSU. In the period under consideration, Alexander Tvardovskii, editor-in-chief of *Novyi mir*, was a member of the Central Committee. Is it conceivable that he was perceived as head of an "anti-establishment coterie"? Is it conceivable that the Politburo would approve for publication a story by, say, Vasilii Aksenov after he deserted the Union of Soviet Writers to join the anti-establishment crowd of *Metropol'*? The Politburo approved

[62]Breslauer, p. xi.

[63]*Ibid.*, p. 17. For more detail, see Notes on Terminology.

[64]*Ibid.*, pp. 130-31.

Solzhenitsyn's story for publication, however reluctantly and under strong pressure from Khrushchev. But still they approved it. The fact is that both *Novyi mir* and the poets and writers whom Breslauer considers anti-establishment—Tvardovskii, Yevtushenko, Voznesenskii, Aksenov, and even Solzhenitsyn (his present anti-communist crusade notwithstanding) were at the time under discussion part of the establishment. Not only would Solzhenitsyn, soon after the publication of *One Day in the Life of Ivan Denisovich*, become a member of the Union of Soviet Writers and be introduced by Khrushchev to the top Soviet elite, but he would seek the highest Soviet literary award—the Lenin Prize. Thus Solzhenitsyn, if we judge not from his later words but from his actions, invested no small effort in seeking entry into the highest ranks of the Soviet establishment. Nor was Ivan Khudenko—the hero of *this* book—anti-establishment. He was personally acquainted with Khrushchev and a number of Politburo members and was allowed to lead a crucial agricultural experiment that could have changed the fate of the Russian peasantry if Khrushchev had remained in office a few years longer. Need I point out that this is not how anti-establishment elements are treated in the Soviet Union? They may be persecuted; they may be expelled from the Union of Soviet Writers or similar institutions; they may be driven into exile or, at the very least, sent to Gorky, but they are not elevated to membership on the Central Committee, they are not editors of literary or sociopolitical journals, they are not allowed to direct very important economic experiments or to publish whatever they write. In a word, they are outcasts.

Who then were these people under Khrushchev if they were not an "anti-establishment coterie"? In terms of the approach to Soviet political conflict proposed here, they were a manifestation of the basic dualism of Russian political culture, which leads to a permanent split within the Soviet establishment. Unlike conventional sovietology, this approach does not limit the Soviet establishment to its anti-reformist part; it allows for a reformist establishment component as well. It was this reformist establishment whose political and economic views were put into action by people like Khudenko and articulated by the *Novyi mir* "coterie" that Breslauer refers to as "anti-establishment." It was this establishment which Khrushchev, in parting ways with the anti-reformist establishment, failed to consolidate and institutionalize.

In explaining the period of the establishment crisis of 1960-1964, the conventional sovietological approach sees only a conflict between the leader and the establishment, and thus is compelled to use such devices as describing people like Tvardovskii and Yevtushenko (why not Khrushchev himself?) as belonging to an anti-establishment coterie. The alternative approach proposed in this study perceives it as a fundamental conflict between two parts of one Soviet establishment, as an episode of historic significance in the perpetual struggle of Russia versus Russia.

To be sure, the conventional approach makes it easy to explain Khrushchev's downfall: the leader fell as soon as he lost the support of his only possible power base — the Soviet establishment. It is from this concept that the standard description of Khrushchev's last struggle as an erratic search for panaceas, as a desperate — and hopeless — attempt to hold on to power, comes. No matter how strongly the "totalitarian" and "revisionist" schools in sovietology disagree on almost everything else, this is what one hears equally from William Odom and Jerry Hough, from Adam Ulam and George Breslauer. No alternatives to this conventional version were ever offered, to the best of my knowledge. Indeed, they cannot be as long as we continue the analysis in terms of conflict between the leader and the establishment — i.e., as long as we ignore the shift in the leader's power base from the anti-reformist part of the establishment to the reformist part, which is quite obvious in the replacement of party professionals by the managerial elite in rural districts — the most far-reaching of Khrushchev's reforms described here. This shift was also discernible in Khrushchev's turn to the reborn peasant elite and to the chemical industry (perceived as a direct challenge to the "steel-eaters") and in the debate on managerial autonomy. Unlike many of Khrushchev's previous initiatives in the 1950s, these don't look like panaceas. They are rather quite realistic means for the radical transformation of the national economy directly related to the change of elites managing its essential sectors. (These were the first seeds of the reform realized in Hungary in the 1970s.) If it was a search, then it was a search for new constituencies, not panaceas. Khrushchev seemed to have matured as a reformist leader, with his perceptions changed, his strategies evolved. Still not a coherent policymaker, he had been intuitively groping for the essential truth that one cannot base the reform of society on anti-reformist forces. In contrast to

110

most of his previous actions, he seemed to be on the right path—at least judging from Kadar's success with similar reformist initiatives. From this point of view, Khrushchev's last years in office look not like a doomed effort to hold on to power against the will of the Soviet establishment, but rather like a painful and dangerous attempt to break through to a genuine reform.

Chapter 4

POSTSCRIPT TO REFORM

The end of the regime of Reformation, however, didn't spell the immediate end of reforms. The cultural roots of the Russian Reform, as well as the Hungarian impulse given the system by Khrushchev, appeared to be sufficiently profound to prevent the immediate advent of the era of political stagnation. Instead, there was a post-reformist regime (along with a second wave of the Link Reform) which brought a kind of a repetition of the political drama of 1960-1964.

The general outline of events after October 1964 was vaguely reminiscent of what had taken place after the dictator's demise in March 1953, as if history itself tried to give the Reform a fresh start. One of the duumvirs in the post-Khrushchev National Leadership—Aleksey Kosygin—seemed to be destined to repeat the role of Georgy Malenkov with his emphasis on the expansion of consumer industry (Group B). Another member of the Politburo—Gennadii Voronov—tried to replace Khrushchev as a sponsor of the resurrected Link Reform in 1968-1970, no longer as vigorous as it was under the regime of Reform, but still seemingly full of promise.

Kosygin's strategy appeared to reflect the disillusionment of the urban middle management (as well as of the Central Economic Administration, restored in its full glory after Khrushchev's downfall) with Khrushchev's focus on agriculture. The main lesson the victorious provincial elites (then represented in the National Leadership by Leonid Brezhnev) appeared to learn from the establishment crisis was that "money decides everything in agriculture," while the metropolitan elites (represented by Kosygin) seemed to learn precisely the opposite—that capital investment has little or no effect on agriculture. Hence their return to the original (Malenkovist) version of the Reform—i.e., to the "sharp rise" in light industry needed to satisfy the demands of urban consumers. The best description of this "urban-consumerist" strategy can be found in a recent book by George Breslauer:

> Let's not invest very much in agriculture, because the rate of return doubtless will be very low, compared to what we might get from light industry. Agriculture's problems are organizational, in part; but let's admit, our peasants are ill-educated and lazy. You raise their incomes, they work less and get by on the same. They would rather exert themselves on their private plots in any case. So why pour money into the public sector, where the peasant will find ways to avoid hard work whatever the incentive? On the other hand, investment in light industry—if it is tied closely enough to consumer demand—could prove a great source of expansion and rising productivity well into the future. . . . Moreover, the availability of attractive consumer goods (and, perhaps, rising urban affluence in the face of a more slowly growing rural sector) may be just the right spur to much greater rural effort and productivity.[1]

This formulation is Breslauer's own, but it is a reflection of his penetrating insight into Soviet affairs that I heard analogous arguments during 1966-1968 in Moscow from many highly placed managers and journalists, including some editors of influential newspapers and journals. Despite the fact that this approach completely ignored the potential of the Link Reform (in particular, the differentiation of the kolkhoz society and the emergence of a rural elite which was well-educated and industrious—in any case, capable of decisively increasing the productivity of agricultural labor), it contained a promising seed of change, and much could be said in its defense, just as might have been said in defense of Malenkov's strategy of a sharp rise in light industry in 1953. However, as in Malenkov's case, the basic weakness of this approach lay in its political naivete: it threatened the most vital interests of the provincial elites who—along with the "comrades with a hunger for metal"—had just achieved a decisive victory and were once again at the peak of their political power. They had not overthrown the hated Khrushchev in order to return to the policies of the equally despised Malenkov.

[1]Breslauer, p. 142.

True, the adherents of the urban-consumerist strategy emphasized its positive potential—it would lead to a rise in living standards in the cities, it would reduce the dangerously high money supply in the hands of the general population (thereby lessening the danger of inflation), and it would stimulate an increase in labor productivity in industry (and indirectly in the countryside). However, its opponents had quite different things on their minds. First of all, the urban-consumerist strategy not only would take the already scarce capital away from heavy industry (cherished by "the comrades with a hunger for metal") as well as from agriculture (threatening the positions of the "comrades elected to leadership posts"), but also implied a revision of the Stalinist "general line" (which was dear to the "hidebound dogmatists"). Second, the urban-consumerist strategy challenged the vested interests of the central economic administration—Kosygin's political base—in that it required managerial autonomy and decentralization of the management of the economy. Thus, in the eyes of those groups representing the complete spectrum of Khrushchev's adversaries, Kosygin must have seemed Malenkov's, if not Khrushchev's, heir attempting to rob them of the fruits of their political victory.

It was almost inconceivable that the provincial elites would not find in the ranks of the new National Leadership someone capable of confronting the metropolitan strategy. Once again, as in 1957, it would have to be one of *them*—a peasant's son who had patiently climbed the ladder of the traditional hierarchy, from district to provincial to republican committees and then to the top. Moreover, it was inconceivable that this leader would not advance an alternative to Kosygin's urban-consumerist strategy which would be as similar as two peas in a pod to the one that Khrushchev counterposed to Malenkov's strategy in 1954-1957. In just that way Leonid Brezhnev gave center stage to agriculture and the military, relying on the already tested alliance of the "comrades elected to leadership posts," the "hidebound dogmatists," and "steel-eaters" under the aegis of the resurrected "general line." Under these conditions, the urban-consumerist strategy was doomed beforehand, even though the Plenum of September 1965 solemnly announced a program of economic reform in which managerial autonomy and "horizontal relations between enterprises"—the Soviet euphemism for market—would be key features.

Brezhnev's approach to agriculture is described by Breslauer as "financial" (as distinct from Khrushchev's, which he calls "organizational"). The Plenum of March 1965 projected for 1966-1970 an investment of 71 billion rubles in the countryside—an amount unprecedented in Soviet history, and as much as the state had invested in agriculture over the entire postwar period. Subsequent capital investment in agriculture would be even more impressive. For the decade 1965-1975, it would exceed everything that had been invested in the countryside during the preceding fifty years of the Soviet regime. Furthermore, during this period the increase in investment in agriculture would exceed the increase in investment in the military. In 1980 the investment would reach 37 billion rubles—that is, 27 percent of all Soviet investment. But the pouring of these gigantic sums into the kolkhoz barrel since Khrushchev's downfall obscures the real aims of the Brezhnevist strategy.

The hypothesis proposed here is that these huge sums of money were primarily intended—in line with the desires of the provincial elites—*to eliminate the link alternative*. They were to be used to show that the kolkhoz system was viable in the form in which it had existed since Stalin's time, and thereby solidify the power of the little Stalins over the countryside. The money was only a means to achieve this end, and it was only part of the Brezhnevist strategy, which was a well thought out series of measures for preserving the countryside in its kolkhoz form.

This strategy also included removing the limitations on the size of private plots of the kolkhoz members (and later even stimulating their expansion), the liquidation of a considerable portion of the kolkhoz debts, raising the procurement prices for kolkhoz produce, decreasing the required deliveries by the kolkhoz to the state, and most important—the deeply cherished dream of the little Stalins—overtaking the United States in farm tractors by increasing their number in the kolkhozy to 5 million. Thus the Brezhnevist strategy for the countryside is perhaps best described as a bribe paid to the provincial elites—a gigantic state subsidy which would make it possible for them to suppress the link movement, and thereby halt completely the process of de-Stalinization of the countryside. In this sense, Brezhnev's strategy could be designated the "kolkhoz strategy."

KHUDENKO'S MEMORANDUM

In the fall of 1964, Ivan Khudenko sent Khrushchev a memorandum on general reconstruction of the Soviet countryside. (Khrushchev does not mention the memorandum in his memoirs, which suggests that he did not have time to read it.) This memorandum was the most forceful statement of the Link Reform known to me and, we might say, Khudenko's political testament to the country which rejected his ideas, but which nevertheless remained dearer to him than anything on earth. Unfortunately, no copy of this memorandum has survived. I will attempt here to summarize its contents as well as I can remember them.[2]

Khudenko began by arguing that the entire agricultural strategy of the USSR since 1928—that is, from the time of Stalin's turn to collectivization—was fundamentally misguided since in all its aspects—from the expansion of the cultivated area to the organization of labor, wages, and mechanization—it moved in directions opposite to other modern societies. For example, the cultivated area in the USSR almost doubled in size between 1928 and 1962—from 113 million hectares to 216 million. During the same period the cultivated area was reduced in the United States from 169 million hectares to 116, at which time the production of Soviet agriculture was much less that of American agriculture. Furthermore, despite the expansion of cultivated area, the annual growth rate of Soviet agricultural production was falling—from 5 percent in the 1950s to 3 percent in the 1960s. The increase in labor productivity was also declining—from 2 percent in the 1950s to 1 percent in the 1960s. If these tendencies continued—and the retention of the Stalinist kolkhoz system appeared to make it inevitable—then in the 1970s, Khudenko predicted, labor productivity and agricultural production would stop increasing, regardless of capital investment.

There is no reason to think (said Khudenko) that we in the USSR need more cultivated area per capita than the Americans. A sharp reduction in the cultivated area (to perhaps 100 million hectares) would make it possible to concentrate agricultural production in the regions with the most fertile soils and favorable climates, which would

[2]I was able to insert some ideas from this memorandum into my articles. See, for example, "Trevogi Smolenshchiny."

afford the most efficient production. This would put an end to one of the most unfortunate legacies of Stalin—the overextension of the Soviet countryside—and open the way for the intensification of agricultural labor. For the working of 100 million hectares we would not need the 2.5 million tractors we now have, and certainly not 5 million, as in America. We have no need to ape others. We need no more tractors than we have link tractor drivers (assuming that we do away with the second most unfortunate Stalinist legacy—the "facelessness" of the land implicit in the kolkhoz system). Ten thousand field-crop links (with 10 tractors each) on 3,000 link enterprises—in place of 50,000 kolkhozy and sovkhozy—could produce as much grain as American farmers produce. For this we would need only 100,000 tractors. Insofar as kolkhozy remain, they would need another 150,000. Altogether it would take 250,000 tractors—one-tenth of what we already have.[3] (To appreciate the magnitude of Khudenko's "heresy," it is important to know that the USSR produces about 300,000 tractors every year—more than America, England, and West Germany combined.)

But we must bear in mind—Khudenko continued—that the tractors we produce in the USSR are about the worst in the world. They need major overhauling after only 4,000 hours in the field (while American tractors need overhauling after 6,000 hours), and they last only half as long as American tractors. Our tractors do not last long because they are made in plants with equipment designed to be converted at any moment to the production of tanks. Our agricultural machine-building works as it did in Stalin's time under the slogan "If there is war tomorrow." Tanks do not need to be long lasting, but tractors do. We have almost no specialized trucks capable of carrying out specifically agricultural functions. We do not have them because our trucks are made to transport soldiers, not potatoes. We produce more tractors than we need because the capacity of our agricultural

---

[3]At this point Khudenko was clearly exaggerating. The huge territory of Kazakhstan, on which he based his calculations, may not require—under the Link Reform—more than a single tractor driver for 1,000 hectares, but in other soil zones of the USSR the situation is different. Even if we take 250 hectares as the average work allotment per tractor driver—as was determined in 1976 in Stavropol' territory, when the link movement was revived there (*Ekonomicheskaia gazeta*, 1976, No. 20, p. 18)—no more than 400,000 tractors would be needed, not the millions proposed by supporters of the "general line."

machine-building industry is determined by its potential as defense industry. For the same reason our planners keep repeating "Steel! Steel!" like parrots, and resisting the expansion of our petrochemical industries: tanks are not made of plastic, only of steel. By combining civilian and military functions in this way, our agricultural machine-building industry fulfills both of them poorly. A sharp reduction in the output of tractors would put an end to a third unfortunate legacy of Stalin—the militarization of agricultural machine-building.

A twofold reduction in cultivated area and a tenfold reduction in the output of tractors would cut the expenditures of the state on agriculture by about two-thirds. Reducing the cost of production of agricultural produce in the links (by a factor of four or five) would cut them even more. (Khudenko cited precise figures, but unfortunately I don't remember them.) This would lead both to a radical decline in the prices of agricultural produce in the cities (and thereby to a rise in the general standard of living of the population), and to a sharp decrease in government procurement prices, which now constitute a state subsidy for the artificial support of the kolkhoz system. The link enterprises would eliminate the need to spend hard currency on grain and meat, as happened in 1963. The money now invested in the kolkhoz system, which is incapable of intensive use of either the land or equipment, is essentially being thrown out the window. No other country allows itself to spend for nothing the immense sums of capital we spend to retain the Stalinist tradition of maximum party intervention in agriculture, which looks especially ridiculous after the anti-Stalinist 20th and 22nd party congresses. It is more than ridiculous—it is criminal, if we bear in mind the real needs of the countryside, which we have neglected for decades. Just look at our country roads, which are worse than they were in tsarist Russia. We have about a million kilometers of unpaved roads which are transformed into swamps just when we need to haul out the harvest, as a result of which a considerable part of the gathered harvest is spoiled. The money saved by the state by reducing procurement prices and tractor output should go toward the construction of a modern agricultural infrastructure, for we do not have the paved roads or the modern equipment necessary for the mechanization of animal husbandry and the producing, processing, storage, and marketing of agricultural produce.

When people say that in America a total of 5 million farmers feed the country, they are ignoring the fact that 7 million more are employed in the preliminary phases of agri-business as suppliers of goods and services to agriculture. And there are 11 million more employed in processing, storing, and marketing agricultural produce. Both of these stages of agri-business in the United States are clearly separated from the agricultural production proper, and are extremely capital-intensive, which results in a very high labor productivity ratio for agriculture.

The Link Reform would liberate millions of working hands which are needed to create our agri-business and develop the service area. If we wish, however, to retain kolkhozy—on the periphery of the link enterprises (for those who cannot work in the links and do not wish to move to the cities)—we should increase the production of equipment for individual working of the land a hundredfold. If kolkhozy remain, then—since the production of grain would be concentrated in the link enterprises—they should be oriented toward intensifying the production of labor-intensive crops, such as potatoes and other vegetables and fruit, as well as milk and meat. At present, people are working by hand on their private plots, which is a barbaric, Asiatic waste of human labor. (It has been estimated that mechanizing the cultivation of potatoes on private plots would save one billion man-days every year.)

Precisely at this moment (Khudenko admonished Khrushchev at the conclusion of his memorandum) when, thanks to the 1962 reforms, the rural districts have ceased to exist, and the rural provincial committees are so caught up in the struggle with their colleagues in industry that their resistance to change can only be minimal, the political conditions for the introduction of the Link Reform are more favorable than they have been at any time. We have waited for these conditions since 1928. If we let this moment go, we will probably have to wait at least another decade. And we have no more decades left. The abandonment of the Link Reform will almost certainly lead to the stagnation of the Soviet countryside through the 1970s. Even worse, it will likely lead to a permanent, humiliating—for a country with such enormous agricultural potential—dependence on foreign grain.

Such, in general terms, was the comprehensive plan for the de-Stalinization of the Soviet countryside suggested by one of the most prominent leaders of reformist Russia in the 1960s. Although it was

119

in many respects compatible with the urban-consumerist strategy of Kosygin, it was clearly inconsistent with the kolkhoz strategy of Brezhnev. Whereas Khudenko's plan envisaged a lowering of the procurement prices for agricultural produce (which would immediately have shown the inability of the kolkhozy to compete with the link enterprises), the Brezhnev plan envisaged the raising of these prices. Whereas Khudenko was proposing full industrialization of agricultural labor, Brezhnev's plan was oriented toward the isolation of the kolkhozniks on their private plots which—given the near total lack of small-scale power tools in the Soviet countryside—was an orientation toward hand labor. Whereas Khudenko proposed a sharp reduction in the output of tractors, Brezhnev wanted to increase tractor production. Whereas Khudenko's plan was aimed at the de-militarization of agricultural machine-building, the plan of the Brezhnevist alliance of the military and the provincial elites was oriented toward its intensification. In other words, the kolkhoz and link strategies were fundamentally opposed. Brezhnev had to regard Khudenko as an enemy. Under these conditions it is not surprising that Brezhnev took a personal part in the reprisal against Khudenko by ordering Kunaev, the first secretary of the central committee of the party in Kazakhstan, to give him up to be crushed by the local little Stalins.[4]

THE TRAGIC PROPHECY

But Khudenko turned out to be a prophet. He was not only correct in predicting the stagnation of the Soviet countryside through the 1970s if it kept the kolkhoz system (as well as the permanent dependence on purchases of grain from abroad), but he also correctly predicted—and there was something particularly tragic in this prophecy—that if the moment was not seized (in 1962-1964) when the power of the Soviet prefects was at its nadir, it would become politically impossible to introduce the Link Reform. Therein he predicted the collapse of the second wave of the Link Reform in 1968-1970, of which he himself was one of the chief architects. Therein he predicted his own downfall.

[4]This at least is how the matter was interpreted by one of Kunaev's speech-writers.

The leader of the second wave—Gennadii Voronov—did not have even one hundredth of Khrushchev's influence. The rural managerial elite suffered a crushing defeat in its struggle with the Soviet prefects. All the conflicts, problems, and resistances known to us from the history of the first wave of the Link Reform were repeated the second time around. But there was no longer a Khrushchev to whom appeal might be made, who might be capable of a political breakthrough. In the sphere of ideas the link movement was marching in place.

Khudenko, the lonely knight, continued the struggle in Akchi against all odds. Not a single kolkhoz chairman followed his lead. What could be done to help Khudenko? Scientific conferences were convened; polemical articles were written; a beautiful documentary film about Akchi was made, but it remains buried in the film archives; a play was written about Khudenko, but it was given only one performance. Nothing helped. On the day after the performance of the play, Khudenko was arrested with two of his colleagues.[5]

I am proud that I proved to be one of the few allies of Khudenko who supported him to the end. When he was under investigation, when Akchi was closed and had been barbarously pillaged, when the place where one of the most heroic reform experiments in Soviet history had been conducted—a kind of new New Lanark of a new Robert Owen—was condemned to become a desert again, when a great many people had fallen silent either from fright or from loss of hope—I succeeded in publishing the last panegyric to Akchi, and in paying a final tribute to a great Russian reformer.[6] In the fall of 1974, Khudenko died in prison. He died of a broken spirit. A man of passionate temperament, he could not live long in a cage, just as Alexander Tvardovskii and Nikita Khrushchev did not live long after being removed from their offices. Almost the only thing we know about him after his arrest in 1973 is that in court he stood firm, not only proclaiming his innocence but accusing his accusers. In addition we know that before his death this big, husky man weighed only 100 pounds. Like Khrushchev and Tvardovskii he was extinguished by grief, by humiliation,

[5]My report of this shameful episode is used by Hedrick Smith in his book *The Russians* (Quadrangle, 1976), pp. 212-14.

[6]"Dvizhenie molodogo geroia" [The movement of the young hero], *Novyi mir*, 1972, No. 7; "Kino i nauchno-tekhnicheskaia revolutsiia" [Films and the revolution in science and technology], *Iskusstvo kino*, 1972, No. 11.

by loss of hope. Finally, we know that Russia still pays a heavy price for these political murders.

THE FATE OF THE VICTORS

What about those who committed the murders, however? What about Brezhnev and Kosygin, who claimed that theirs was a genuine reformist regime purged of the "harebrained" and "voluntaristic," populist and utopian Khrushchevist admixtures? Did they live happily ever after with their reforms?

As we now know, both Kosygin's scheme, with its emphasis on managerial autonomy (1965-1969), and Brezhnev's program, with its emphasis on production associations (1970-1973), would be dissolved in the political stagnation which followed. More than that, it is easy to see that their reformist efforts were lost causes even before they began (one reason why I call 1965-1974 a post-reformist decade).

Though Khrushchev was unable to create a new reformist constituency, he at least realized that a great reform cannot be founded on an anti-reformist power base. Even if he was inconsistent, he at least moved in the right direction, splitting the two Russias—the reformist and the anti-reformist—and positioning them for a decisive battle. He declared war on the anti-reformist elites and fought them with an artfulness much greater than any other Russian reformist leader in the twentieth century: certainly greater than Stolypin in the 1900s, or Lenin after 1921, or Bukharin in the 1920s, not to mention Malenkov and Kosygin. Setting the party professionals, for example, against the Central Economic Administration, he nearly destroyed the latter in 1957. Then, playing the "reformist" generals of the strategic forces against the "conservative" commanders of conventional troops, he moved to reduce military expenditures. In 1962, backed by the rural managerial elite, he punished the party professionals, eliminating the district level party branches in the rural areas. Setting the rural prefects against their urban counterparts at the provincial level, and thus undermining their powerful caucus in the "parliament," he tried to destroy the power of the provincial elites. He invited people from all walks of life to participate in parliamentary sessions, especially representatives from the peasant elite, academics, and rural managers. He played the *Novyi mir* party against the "priestly" hierarchy, undermining the very foundation of the Stalinist "general line." Although he eventually lost his struggle, he clearly established himself as one of the great Russian reformist leaders, whereas Kosygin and Brezhnev for all their reformist ambitions will remain forever symbols of political stagnation.

The concept of *establishment reconciliation* which Kosygin and Brezhnev devised to counter Khrushchev's "harebrained schemes" couldn't help but fail. They were asking the impossible, trying to reconcile the irreconcilable: to combine a rise in the living standards of the population with an ambitious effort "to rearm Russia" (to develop "butter" and "guns" at the same time), and to attempt to rationalize the life of the country with a concerted effort to deliberalize it. They proclaimed decentralization in industry while restoring the power of the Central Economic Administration, whose primary interest was blocking industrial reform. They tolerated the second wave of the Link Reform while allying themselves with the Soviet prefects, whose primary interest was blocking agricultural reform. They tried to expand the civilian sector of the economy while diverting the resources it needed to the arms industry in order to keep peace with the military. They proclaimed their tolerance of Soviet Protestantism while pacifying the Soviet "priesthood," intensifying censorship, harassing the dissident movement, and putting an end to the *Novyi mir* party and with it the Khrushchevist era of cultural liberalization. In short, they based their reforms on anti-reformist constituencies and expected them to succeed.

It is doubtful that they ever understood what was happening to them—the failure of all their plans which looked so sober and moderate, so totally devoid of Khrushchev's intemperate outbursts, and yet were leading nowhere. Whatever they touched appeared to turn out the opposite of what they had intended. They wanted the nation to move again, but they produced stagnation. They wanted abundance, but they produced scarcity. They wanted detente with the West, but they produced confrontation. Perhaps we will never know how they felt being trapped in this paradoxical situation, and not even able to explain to themselves the cause of their failures. They presided over a rotten regime which victimized them as mercilessly as they had victimized Ivan Khudenko, Nikita Khrushchev, Alexander Tvardovskii, and Andrey Sakharov—victims who are among the most poignant figures in the tragic history of Russia in the twentieth century. There was no doubt a kind of poetic justice in their fate, but it also illustrated the inherent cruelty of the Russian political system.

EPILOGUE?

Could things have turned out differently if Khudenko had written his memorandum a year earlier, and if he had been able to ignite Khrushchev with his ideas? When he was still in power at *Novyi mir*, would Tvardovskii have succeeded in doing for Khudenko what he did for Solzhenitsyn if he had embraced Khudenko's ideas in the 1960s? Could the Soviet 1960s have ended differently if the three great reformers—the writer, the politician, and the ideologist—had met and understood each other in time? Is there any sense now in speculating—when none of this happened, when we already know how this drama ended?

But do we know? Is it certain that everything which Khudenko, Khrushchev, and Tvardovskii did for the Russian countryside has disappeared without a trace and forever? Can we know that the ideas of the Soviet 1960s will never be revived? Strange things happen in history—and in Russian history they happen particularly often. Let me say only that while the demographic tendencies in the 1970s worked *against* the Link Reform, in the 1980s they will work *for* it. We know now that from 1971 to 1978 the number of people employed in the economy in the USSR grew by 15.8 million—that is, increased by two million a year. There was a huge increase in the population of working age, contrary to expectations; from 1976 to 1980 it increased by 11.2 million people. However, during the current five-year plan, it will grow by only 3.3 million, and in the period 1986-1990, there will be practically no growth.[7] Thus, for the first time in Soviet history, the additional human resources needed for the Stalinist extensive strategy for development of the economy will be lacking. Together with the food crisis—which during the 1970s, as Khudenko had predicted, became chronic—this will work for the ideas of the 1960s. Will the impact of these changes be sufficient for the resurrection of those ideas? Consider the fact that the previously obscure Mikhail

[7]V. Perevedentsev, "Na perelome" [At the turning point], *Literaturnaia gazeta*, 11/26/80.

Gorbachev, the former first secretary of the Stavropol territorial committee, who introduced the Link Reform in his territory in 1976 (without success, of course), was suddenly promoted in 1980 to the Politburo and given responsibility for Soviet agriculture. Will he play the role of a new Voronov? Or a new Khrushchev? Or is Gregory Grossman right when he says that "now, perhaps, it is too late and [Soviet] institutions are perhaps too ossified and the vested interests are too strong for the system to be reformed in the normal way—without cataclysm"?[8] Who can know? Each of us has his own limits of patience and his own limits of hope. For Khudenko they were reached in 1974; for Grossman (it seems) in 1980. Could both of them have been wrong?

[8]"The Economics of Virtuous Haste" (Bernard Moses Memorial Lecture, Berkeley, May 19, 1980).

NOTES ON TERMINOLOGY

SOVIET PROTESTANTISM

Even in our ecumenical age Martin Luther remains excommunicated from the Roman Catholic church, Protestants in Northern Ireland still refuse to live on the same streets with Catholics, and the Shiite Muslims still hate the Sunnis. In the Middle Ages this alienation between peoples belonging to different branches or sub-ideologies of one meta-ideological creed, like Christianity or Islam, was much stronger, as is generally acknowledged by most historians. On the other hand, it is also generally acknowledged that Communism, with its claim to be the wave of the future, is a secular religion. Many authorities go so far as to admit basic differences between Euro-Communism and, say, Albanian Communism, but when it comes to the analysis of Soviet Communism, the same authorities refuse to accept the argument that it also represents essentially a meta-ideology reminiscent of medieval Christianity or Islam, and as such has sub-ideologies not only different but antithetical—like Protestantism and Catholicism.

This refusal to differentiate between antithetical branches of Soviet Communist meta-ideology seems all the more strange in the light of Russian history, in which it has not been uncommon for major reforms to include not only basic institutional or economic changes but also a comprehensive split within a prevailing meta-ideology—a split related to practically all spheres of life, including fundamental beliefs and moral values. It is enough to mention the sixteenth-century split between the Josephites and the Non-Acquirers (the latter were the closest the Russian church ideologists came to Protestantism) or the nineteenth-century split between the Westernizers and the Slavophiles.

In any case, the post-Stalin Soviet reform was no exception: the entire hierarchy of moral imperatives changed, sometimes beyond recognition. Khrushchev's reformist sub-ideology was in many ways the antithesis of the Stalinist sub-ideology of dictatorship. For the latter, belief in the inevitability of a new world war had been an imperative conditioning belief in the all-saving capacity of the Father of the Fatherland, but the reformist sub-ideology dropped both imperatives. The major values of the dictatorship sub-ideology were paternalist, ascetic, isolationist, and anti-consumerist, with the fundamental imperative of national survival invoked to justify all sacrifices. The values of the reformist sub-ideology were directly opposed to the ethos of this National-Communist sub-ideology.

To clarify this point, let me begin with an example. By now it is common knowledge that a severe food crisis plagues the Soviet citizenry—that meat is a very rare commodity in Soviet stores, and food rationing is becoming a way of life in the USSR. Even Brezhnev acknowledged publicly that the food situation is a major political problem for the Soviet regime. The "food program" was the first priority with Andropov as well. Now anyone who knows anything about Soviet history would be hard-pressed to comprehend what the fuss is all about. If one compares present-day food production in the USSR to that under Stalin's dictatorship, it is evident that the food situation has dramatically improved in recent decades. Grain production has more than doubled, and the production of meat has tripled. Yet no one ever thought of the food situation in Stalin's empire as a crisis—at least not the imperial leadership. There was no hint of instituting a special food program, nor did it occur to anyone that food might constitute a major political problem for the regime. Why?

Let us look for a moment at some statistics. In 1913, before the Revolution, Russia produced 86 million tons of grain and 5 million tons of meat. Forty years later, at the end of Stalin's dictatorship, food production had declined to 81 million tons of grain and 4.9 million tons of meat while the population was significantly larger. How had the Soviet people survived the dictatorship?

One food staple had increased in production during all those years, almost tripling—from 31 million tons before the Revolution to 81 million tons in 1950. I am referring to potatoes—the bread and meat of the Russian poor. If we don't include grass (weeds, dead-nettle, and goose-foot), which the peasants were also eating in Stalin's time, there can hardly be any doubt that the decades of the dictatorship were survived on potatoes. People were hungry, poorly dressed, and crowded into communal apartments and barracks, and yet they seemed to be content—at least no one heard them talking about a food crisis. How could such conditions be tolerated in one of the greatest modern nations in the middle of the twentieth century? Clearly this couldn't be accomplished by terror alone: people agreed to bear these material hardships as long as they were perceived as imperative for national survival in the impending world war. In addition the nation was given the spiritual excitement of an unprecedented imperial aggrandizement with a charismatic *vozhd'*—a deified Father at the top who could console all grievances, dry all tears. It is this Orwellian combination of national survival and imperial aggrandizement which is National-Communism, the sub-ideology of dictatorship.

One fine day, however, the Russian God died. And as if awakening from a long dream, people looked around and suddenly found themselves in a desert. Nikita Khrushchev, instead of trying to put the confused nation back to sleep, came forward to mercilessly expose the dead God as an idol and the most ruthless tyrant in history, who held power by an axe. From the point of view of his opponents—the Stalinists—this was Khrushchev's greatest sin. Suddenly there was an end to the anti-consumerism, paternalism, and isolationism. Khrushchev promised meat to the hungry and modern apartments to the barracks dwellers. Not only did he end the isolationism of National-Communism, but he opened the world to the Soviet elites and made it possible for them to compare their own and Western lifestyles. He rejected the fundamental National-Communist notion of the inevitability of a new world war, and scarcity was no longer accepted as an imperative for national survival. The empire suddenly ceased to be a closed and self-contained Orwellian universe, becoming instead part of an open and interdependent world.

Khrushchev unleashed a dynamic and uncontrollable process of rising consumer expectations, shattering the totalitarian sub-ideology. He proposed instead a strikingly different social contract—an unwritten Magna Carta of the post-totalitarian era—which, in contrast to the past, implicitly linked the legitimacy of the new reformist regime to the steady rise of living standards of the people.

As Khrushchev well understood, the new contract required a major overhaul of all aspects of national life. The gun-oriented Stalinist economy of the garrison state had to be transformed into a butter-oriented economy; the civilian sector had to be expanded at the expense of the military; military expenditures had to be significantly reduced; the strict censorship had to be relaxed and major areas of life depoliticized; the strategy of confrontation in world politics had to be replaced with a strategy of detente; the fundamental priorities of the system had to be shifted from external—i.e., "the revolutionary transformation of the world"—to internal—i.e., "the welfare of the state," which, Khrushchev would say, "is determined by the quantity of products that men receive and consume."

The new Consumerist-Communist sub-ideology no longer assumed that the superiority of socialism could be taken for granted, as it was under National-Communism. In good Calvinist fashion, it had to be proved by practical performance. Only by overtaking the capitalist world in economic output and labor productivity—that is, only by success in open economic competition with the West—could socialism make certain that history is on its side. This success could be measured in precise economic terms, which put an end to the kinds of communist mysticism that flourished under National-Communism, thereby greatly diminishing the role of the Soviet "priesthood"—i.e., the professional interpreters of the divine truth imperceptible to ordinary humans. To be sure, socialism was still perceived as the "highest truth" in the new credo, but the role of the "priestly" hierarchy as mediator between the truth and believers was changed. Secular experts, academics, economists, and sociologists, as well as writers and literary critics, were allowed to compete with the "priesthood." The cultural establishment was split into two factions represented by two Moscow journals—*Novyi mir* and *Oktiabr'*.

And as during the Protestant Reformation, the petrified official doctrine was mercilessly compared to the original "scriptures" of Lenin and Marx—compared and condemned. In a word, what occurred was a demythologization or secularization of socialism. In the 1920s, during a previous Reformation, Nikolai Bukharin—the Soviet Luther—expressed essentially the same Protestant credo: "If the party does not create better conditions of life for the people than existed before the revolution, then the people are entitled to ask: "Why did you play this hellish music called revolution?" In the 1960s Khrushchev would unwittingly echo this, not suspecting whom he echoed: "Our country strikes fear into the capitalist world . . . not because the Soviet Union is the strongest state in a military sense but because socialism creates better life for the people."

All of this taken together—the rejection of the priestly hierarchy as the principal mediator between the Truth and Man, the demythologization of the Truth, fearless reliance on figures and practical results as indications of God's support—provides the basis for referring to this new Consumerist-Communist credo as Soviet Protestantism. In addition, it is closely related both to the phenomenon of Russian Reformation and to the medieval character of the Soviet empire. Just as the removal or relaxation of institutional barriers such as serfdom or collectivization stimulates the process of peasant differentiation which is the subject of this book, so with the removal of the dictatorship Soviet communism loses its mono-ideological character. As in the 1920s it becomes a meta-ideology. An ideological differentiation analogous to the social and political differentiations of the reformist era takes place, allowing for antithetical sub-ideologies to emerge, with Soviet Protestantism the most prominent among them.

POST-TOTALITARIAN STATE

The criterion used here for distinguishing different authoritarian regimes is their capacity for political change. From this point of view, totalitarianism is an extreme case in which the regime is capable of arresting all political change. In order to be capable of this, it is not enough for a regime to be a combination of terroristic police control, a monopolistic ideology with chiliastic claims, and a monopolistic political party—as most definitions of totalitarianism seem to imply. A Father of the Fatherland is needed as well—an all-powerful, charismatic leader, a kind of Pied Piper of Hamelin able to lead the children away into hell, be he Hitler or Stalin, Mao or Khomeini. It is this that constitutes the strongest appeal of modern totalitarianism and at the same time is its Achilles' heel. It introduces a dimension lacking in the ancient despotic state—the only other political system capable of arresting all political change for centuries, sometimes for millennia—i.e., the time dimension. Because of this, modern totalitarianism is unable to perpetuate political stagnation for centuries: in fact it cannot survive the demise of its charismatic leader. If it is militarily defeated, it is open for very radical political modernization, as happened in Germany and Italy after World War II. Otherwise, after the demise of its charismatic leader, it is transformed into a transitional state which I call "post-totalitarian," marked by de-Stalinization (in Russia) or de-Maoization (in China) or—presumably— "de-Castroization" (in Cuba) or "de-Khomeinization" (in Iran). The "post-totalitarian" state is a far cry from ordinary authoritarianism: it remains open to totalitarian restoration, and it still retains the monopolistic political party of its predecessor. However, since it has lost the other tools of totalitarian stagnation—terroristic police control, and, most important, the Father of the Fatherland—it is unable to eliminate the sources of internal political dynamics and reform. This is why I see it as transitional: unlike totalitarianism it is open for either political modernization or totalitarian restoration.

Notes on Terminology

SOVIET "PARLIAMENT"

George Breslauer refers to "two types of kremlinological analysis [which] have dominated the field. One variant looked upon the game of politics in the Kremlin as an entirely opportunistic, Byzantine power struggle. Policies were embraced or abandoned in order to outflank or discredit rivals. The second variant . . . postulated . . . that leaders struggle as well over their personal definitions of what ought to be done to deal with economic, social, and broader political problems" (*Khrushchev and Brezhnev as Leaders*, pp. 8-9). However hard a lay person might find it to believe, this modest move from focusing exclusively on "Byzantine power struggle" to the analysis of "policy preferences" of various Soviet leaders must be considered major progress in sovietology, which in the 1930s-1950s more or less unanimously reduced the enormously complex spectrum of the Russian political *system* to one of its several *regimes* — the dictatorial (or totalitarian). No doubt the world of the dictatorship was almost entirely consumed by Byzantine cunning, but already in 1953-1956 — i.e., immediately after Stalin's demise — it was impossible to explain the intricacies of the political game in Moscow exclusively in these terms. Still it took a decade or so for a "basic split between students of Soviet elite politics" to occur (*ibid.*, p. 17). Even now, two decades after the split, many venerable scholars try to assess the post-totalitarian state with the help of analytical tools of the bygone dictatorial era as if nothing had happened. This stubbornness of what I call the "totalitarian" school of sovietology, quite natural in those who once dominated the field, is not the main problem, however. The main problem as I see it is that the new "revisionist" school didn't go far beyond interpreting political "initiatives [in the Soviet government] through an oligarchic perspective" (*ibid.*, p. 17), that it still "identified the policy preferences of the leader by studying his statements and patterns of behavior, and by comparing these with the statements and apparent political preferences of *other members of the Politburo*" (*ibid.*, p. 9; emphasis added). While allowing for the existence and influence of a "political elite" or a "political establishment" (by which it understands mainly the local, regional, and central officials of the party and state apparatus), the revisionist school still shares the totalitarianists' view that the final word in Soviet policymaking belongs to a small oligarchy at the top which, in Leonard Schapiro's words, "with no elections to fear, with no public opinion or independent courts of law to consider, and with ultimate control over all livelihood, can ignore all pressures brought to bear on it with impunity" (*New York Review of Books*, 7/19/79, p. 8).

This notion of an all-powerful oligarchy squares well with the "Byzantine power struggle" of the dictatorship, but it does not fit with the revisionist thesis that "leaders struggle . . . over their personal definitions of what ought to be done to deal with economic, social, and broader political problems." This suggests the likelihood of conflict within the oligarchy — or even a split, such as occurred in April 1925 or July 1928 or June 1967. What happens in a situation of conflict or of a split within the oligarchy? Abdurakhman Avtorkhanov reports what happened in 1954 when Nikita Khrushchev first proposed the idea of bringing virgin lands under cultivation: "The Presidium of the Central Committee considered this plan fantastic and rejected it. Khrushchev then called the Plenum of the Central Committee [which] supported the idea and ... adopted a resolution proposed by him for its implementation" (*Posev* 7, 1979, p. 23). Seweryn Bialer recalls a similar conflict in 1955 when Khrushchev proposed a trip to Belgrade. That conflict was resolved in the same way: the oligarchy yielded to the decision of the Plenum. Jerry Hough describes a Plenum of February 13, 1957, which literally demolished a decision made by the oligarchy in December 1956. Everything reported about the political struggle in Russia under the reformist regime (1953-1964), which was unusual in Soviet terms for its openness, suggests that the parties struggling within the oligarchy were always very conscious of the presence of the Plenum. At one of the sessions of the Presidium, "Malenkov declared to Nikita Sergeevich: 'Why are you trying to scare us with the Plenum? The Plenum is our home; we will go and explain everything to the Plenum.' But this was not so. They were afraid of the Plenum" (*XXII S'ezd Kommunisticheskoi Partii Sovetskogo Soiuza. Stenograficheskii otchet* [The 22d Congress of CPSU. Stenographic report], (Moscow, 1962), v. 1, p. 106). No doubt Schapiro is correct when he says that the oligarchy has no elections to fear, and no public opinion or independent courts of law to consider. And yet it appears that the "all-powerful oligarchy" must consider the Plenum before going ahead with its decisions (which can be overruled by the Plenum), and that there are pressures brought to bear on it which it cannot ignore. (The political massacre of June 1957 in which the Plenum drove the majority of the oligarchy into political oblivion seems to be a sufficient reminder of the possible consequences of ignoring it.)

The totalitarianists make only vague efforts to explain this "Kremlin revolt." For example, Schapiro says: "The drastic economic reorganization of May 1957 aroused opposition among powerful classes of Soviet society" (*The Communist Party of the Soviet Union* [London: Eyre and Spottiswoode, 1970], p. 556). Elsewhere he acknowledges that "his [Khrushchev's] victory ... was due to real support for his views which he could muster in the Central Committee" (*ibid.*, pp. 560-61). But where had these "powerful classes" come from all of a sudden in a society totally controlled by an all-powerful oligarchy? And why did this oligarchy which "can ignore all the pressures brought to bear on it with impunity" become at the moment of a split an impotent toy in the hands of the Plenum of the Central Committee, which for this reason I call the "Soviet Parliament"?

What the totalitarianists view as "Khrushchev's victory," I see as a victory of the "parliamentary majority." Hough gives the precise count: "There were 19 central industrial administrators among the voting members of the Central Committee, compared with 70 republican, state, and Party officials and regional party secretaries—53 per sent of the voting membership—who would benefit from industrial reorganization directly" (Jerry F. Hough and Merle Fainsod, *How the Soviet Union Is Governed* [Cambridge, Mass.: Harvard University Press, 1979], p. 547). The vote in the oligarchy was 4 to 7 against the industrial reorganization, while in the "Parliament" it was 70 to 19 in favor. This settled the matter, and the "parliamentary majority" prevailed over the majority of the oligarchy.

There was something much larger behind this Kremlin revolt than industrial reorganization. "These were dangerous days for our party," recalls one of the rebels of June 1957 (*XXII S'ezd*, v. 1, p. 394). Said another: "An order was given not to admit members of the Central Committee into the Kremlin, and many of us literally found our way illegally into the place where the Presidium was in session" (*ibid.*, v. 2, p. 107). The oligarchy must have been afraid of a Plenum if such an order was issued. It shows clearly that the "parliamentary" role was denied to the Plenum by the post-dictatorial oligarchy of 1953-1957; indeed the oligarchs "raised a terrible noise" when the representatives of various Soviet elites appeared on the scene. "It does not pay to recount what repulsive things they said to the members of the Central Committee when they arrived," asserts another high-ranking rebel. "So can you imagine why? How do the members of the Central Committee dare to approach them?" (*ibid.*, v. 1, p. 106).

Of course everything we know about this Kremlin revolt is from the victors. We haven't heard (and perhaps never will) from the other side. This prevents us from reconstructing the crisis in its entirety. On the other hand, the actions described by the rebels are not the sort they can be proud of. In fact the story they tell is disgraceful—not only about the vanquished oligarchs, but also about the Soviet system in general, including the victors. Apart from Khrushchev's revelations in his secret speech of 1956, we haven't heard anything from the post-Stalin leaders as shameful as this report of the Kremlin revolt. This seems to give the account some credibility. Consider, for example, this statement from a Soviet leader: "We all understand quite well that if in June 1957 the anti-party group had come out on top, it would not have taken account of age or of previous services, and today in this hall there would be many, many delegates missing. Our party would have been subject to new and severe repression, and *many devoted communists would have been thrown into prison or exterminated*" (*ibid.*, v. 3, p. 130; emphasis added).

It is quite clear from this complex mix of hurt feelings, hatred, and fear that something more than a family quarrel was taking place in the Kremlin in the summer of 1957. Just as in St. Petersburg 227 years earlier, when the representatives of the Russian establishment challenged a post-dictatorial oligarchy in precisely the same way, not only the political lives but the physical survival of the participants seemed to be at stake (see my "Drama of the Time of Troubles," *Canadian-American Slavic Studies*, Spring 1978). The essence of both of these political dramas was the same: the oligarchy feared the establishment while the establishment feared the oligarchy. In both cases a kind of institutional guarantee was sought—an establishment "parliament" to prevent the oligarchy from being transformed into a "collective dictatorship." It didn't work in 1730; in 1957 it did. Khrushchev's declaration when he learned that he had lost the vote in the oligarchy deserves to be quoted in full: "I was elected by the Plenum of the Central Committee, and therefore it is up to it to make the decision. As the Plenum decides, that's the way it will be" (*XXII S'ezd*, v. 1. p. 106). He perhaps had no idea that in making this statement he was laying the cornerstone of the post-totalitarian state: it was to be "parliamentary," not "oligarchical." It was a historical moment: with these words the Soviet establishment acquired its Magna Carta and the "Soviet Parliament" its institutional status.

No doubt the "Soviet Parliament" is one of the most peculiar parliamentary bodies in history. Just as the Soviet meta-ideology is reminiscent of medieval Islam, so the Soviet "Parliament" resembles a medieval assembly. It doesn't represent the society at large, only the "estates"—i.e., various Soviet elites. The provincial "bears" who constitute the parliamentary majority spend most of the time in hibernation. They come to life only in the midst of a political crisis, when competing leaders come to them for approval of their programs and have to humbly accept the bears' judgment. It is only at these conflict points, when the National Leadership is divided, that the "big party guns of the Central Committee, the bosses of Sverdlovsk, of Kharkov, of Novosibirsk, of Omsk, of the Donbas and the Kuzbas, the heavy-handed, broadshouldered, square-headed party mechanics" (Harrison Salisbury, *The Gates of Hell* [New York: Random House, 1975], p. 84) from all over the country invade the capital, and the seemingly all-powerful metropolitan establishment yields and at times cracks like a gilded toy in their merciless paws.

METROPOLITAN AND PROVINCIAL ELITES

For the purposes of this study, including the effort to determine the chances for achieving an irreversible Russian reform in the 1980s, the elites of the Soviet post-totalitarian state can be grouped in three sections: one with a reformist potential, a second with vested interests in maintaining the status quo, and a third, potentially counterreformist. At the core of the status quo section are the "provincial elites"—i.e., the peripheral party and state hierarchies which, with their overwhelming voting power in the Soviet "parliament," have dominated the Soviet political scene for virtually all of the three post-Stalin decades. Two rebellions by the "metropolitan elites"—i.e., those in the Moscow establishment whose principal source of corruption is not economic embezzlement but Western lifestyles—against this provincial domination (one under Malenkov in 1953-1954 and the other under Kosygin in 1965-1969) were crushed by Khrushchev and Brezhnev respectively. The primary results of this provincial domination seem to be the present political stagnation and the unprecedented explosion of economic embezzlement, which is the principal source of corruption of the provincial elites.

However, the political dynamics of the post-totalitarian state cannot be reduced to the confrontation of the provincial and metropolitan elites because the latter are deeply divided. Whereas the National Leadership (the Politburo, the Secretariat, and the office of the Secretary-General), along with various metropolitan establishments, the middle managerial class, and the upper strata of the scientific and artistic intelligentsia, seem to have a reformist potential, the military and the central economic administration (the planners and the officials of numerous Moscow ministries) generate a strong counterreformist impulse.

134

BIBLIOGRAPHY OF WORKS CITED

Avtorkhanov, Abdurakhman. "Tselina Brezhneva" [Brezhnev's virgin lands]. *Posev*, 1979, No. 7.

Bloomfield, Lincoln P., Clemens, Walter C., Jr., and Griffith, Franklyn. *Khrushchev and the Arms Race*. Cambridge, Mass.: MIT, 1966.

Breslauer, George W. *Khrushchev and Brezhnev as Leaders*. London: George Allen and Unwin, 1982.

Brzezinski, Zbigniew. "The Soviet Political System: Transformation or Degeneration?," *Problems of Communism*, January-February 1966.

Cleary, J. W. "The Parts of the Party." *Problems of Communism*, July-August 1964.

Conquest, Robert. "After Khrushchev: A Conservative Restoration." *Problems of Communism*, September-October 1963.

Crankshaw, Edward. *Khrushchev: A Career*. New York: Viking Press, 1966.

Fainsod, Merle. "Khrushchev in Retrospect." *Problems of Communism*, January-February 1965.

Hahn, Werner. *The Politics of Soviet Agriculture, 1960-1970*. Baltimore: Johns Hopkins University Press, 1972.

Hough, Jerry. "A Harebrained Scheme in Retrospect." *Problems of Communism*, July-August 1965.

_____. *The Soviet Prefects*. Cambridge, Mass.: Harvard University Press, 1969.

_____, and Fainsod, Merle. *How the Soviet Union Is Governed*. Cambridge, Mass.: Harvard University Press, 1979.

Khrushchev, N. S. *Stroitel'stvo kommunizma v SSSR i razvitie sel'skogo khoziaistva* [The building of communism in the USSR and the development of agriculture]. 8 vols. Moscow: Gospolitizdat, 1962-1964.

Kochetov, Vsevolod. *Sobranie sochinenii* [Collected works]. Moscow: Khudozhestvennaia Literatura, 1973.

Kokashinskii, Vladimir. "Chelovek i ekonomika. Eksperiment v Akchi" [The man and the economy. The experiment at Akchi]. *Literaturnaia gazeta*, 5/21/69.

_____. "Nuzhen li selu krestianin?" [Does the countryside need the peasant?]. In *Propoved' deistviem* [Preaching by action], ed. Kokashinskii. Moscow, 1968.

_____. "Sila v kollektivizme" [The power of collectivism]. *Molodoi kommunist*, 1970, No. 2.

Kozlov, F. R. "Ob izmeneniakh v Ustave KPSS" [On changes in the bylaws of the CPSU]. In *XXII s'ezd Kommunisticheskoi partii Sovetskogo Soiuza*. Moscow: 1962.

Linden, Carl. "Khrushchev and the Party Battle." *Problems of Communism*, September-October 1963.

Lowe, George. *The Age of Deterrence*. Boston: Little, Brown, 1964.

Malenkov, G. M. "Rech' na 5 Sessii Verkhovnogo Soveta SSSR," *Kommunist*, 1953, No. 12.

Matskevich, I. "S nekotorym otkloneniem ot temy" [A little off the point]. *Golos zarubezh'ia* [Voice from abroad], No. 18, 1980.

Meyer, Alfred. "USSR, Incorporated." In *The Development of the USSR: An Exchange of Views*, ed. Donald W. Treadgold. Seattle, 1964.

Mozhaev, V. "Zemlia zhdet" [The land is waiting]. *Oktiabr'*, 1961, No. 1.

Nekipelov, Viktor. "Khleb i bezhentsy," *Kontinent*, 1980. No. 25.

Ovechkin, Valentin. *Izbrannoe* [Selected works]. Tashkent, 1965.

Panin, D. *Zapiski Sologdina* [Sologdin's notes]. Frankfurt-am-Main, 1973.

Perevedentsev, Viktor. "Na perelome" [At the turning point]. *Literaturnaia gazeta*, 11/26/80.

Petrenko, F. "Proizvodstvo—glavnaia sfera partiinogo rukovodstva" [Production is the main sphere of party leadership]. *Partiinaia zhisn'*, 1963, No. 2.

Rebrin, P. "Glavnoe zveno" [The main link]. *Novyi mir*, 1969, No. 4.

Rigby, Thomas H. "The Extent and the Limits of Authority." *Problems of Communism*, September-October 1963.

Safire, William. "Ninotchka and Tatyana." *New York Times*, 12/4/83.

Salisbury, Harrison E. *The Gates of Hell*. New York: Random House, 1975.

Schapiro, Leonard. "Rewriting the Russian Rules." *New York Review of Books*, 7/19/79.

_____. *The Communist Party of the Soviet Union*. Eyre and Spottiswoode: 1970.

Scheer, Robert. *With Enough Shovels*. New York: Random House, 1982.

Shtarberg, I. G. *Kompleksnye mekhanizirovannye brigady i zven'ia* [Complex mechanized brigades and links]. Blagoveshchensk, 1963.

Smith, Hedrick. *The Russians*. New York: Quadrangle, 1976.

Solzhnenitsyn, A. Interview with BBC, February 1979. Published in *Vestnik RkhD* 127, 1979.

_____. *Pis'mo vozhdiam Sovetskogo Soiuza* [Letter to Soviet leaders]. Paris: YMCA Press, 1974.

Strelianyi, A. "Zveno v tsepi" [A link in the chain]. *Novyi mir*, 1969, No. 4.

XXII S'ezd Kommunisticheskoi partii Sovetskogo Soiuza. Stenograficheskii otchet [The 22nd Congress of the CPSU. Stenographic report]. Moscow, 1962.

Ward, Barbara. "Another Chance for the North." *Foreign Affairs*, Winter 1980/ 81.

Yanov, A. "Davaite razberemsia" [Let's analyze the matter]. *Molodoi kommunist*, 1965, No. 5.

_____. "Drama of the Time of Troubles." *Canadian-American Slavic Studies* 12, 1 (Spring 1978).

_____. "Dvizhenie molodogo geroia" [The movement of the young hero]. *Novyi mir*, 1972, No. 7.

_____. "Flight from Theory." *Slavic Review*, Summer 1983.

_____. "Kino i nauchno-tekhnicheskaia revolutsiia" [Films and the revolution in science and technology]. *Iskusstvo kino*, 1972, No. 11.

_____. "Kolkhoznoe sobranie. Sotsiologicheskii ocherk." *Komsomol'skaia pravda*, 7/5/66. English translation: "A Collective Farm Meeting." *International Journal of Sociology* 6, 2-3 (Summer-Fall 1976): 13-23.

_____. "Kostromskoi eksperiment. Sotsiologicheskii ocherk." *Literaturnaia gazeta*, 12/27/67. English translation: "The Kostroma Experiment." *International Journal of Sociology* 6, 2-3 (Summer-Fall 1976): 42-53.

_____. *The Origins of Autocracy. Ivan the Terrible in Russian History*. Berkeley: University of California Press, 1981.

_____. "Pomogite sil'nomu. Sotsiologicheskii ocherk." *Molodoi kommunist*, 1970, No. 2. English translation: "Help the Strong." *International Journal of Sociology* 6, 2-3 (Summer-Fall, 1976): 64-74.

_____. "Spor s predsedatelem." *Literaturnaia gazeta*, 8/7/68. English translation: "A Dispute with the Chairman." *International Journal of Sociology* 6, 2-3 (Summer-Fall 1976): 54-63.

_____. "Trevogi Smolenshchiny. Sotsiologicheskii ocherk." *Literaturnaia gazeta*, 7/27/66. English translation: "The Tribulations of the Smolensk Countryside." *International Journal of Sociology* 6, 2-3 (Summer-Fall 1976): 24-33.

_____. "V chem oshibaiutsia storonniki 'mozgovogo tresta.' Razmyshleniia o kolkhoznoi demokratii" [Where do the proponents of the "brain trust" make their mistake? Reflections on kolkhoz democracy]. *Literaturnaia gazeta*, 6/4/69.

_____. "Zhivaia praktika i konservatizm myshleniia" [Living practice and conservatism of thought]. *Literaturnaia gazeta*, 4/8/70.

Zhukov, Iu. "Zveno uspekha" [The link of success]. In *Gvardeitsy za rabotoi* [The guardsmen at work], ed. Zhukov. Nal'chik, 1965.

INDEX

ALEXANDER YANOV, born in Odessa, was graduated from Moscow State University in 1953 with a degree in history. He became a political writer, but in 1974 was forced to emigrate from the USSR. He is now Visiting Associate Professor in the Department of Political Science, University of Michigan. He is the author of *The Origins of Autocracy: Ivan the Terrible in Russian History* (University of California Press, 1981), as well as *The Russian New Right* (1978) and *Detente After Brezhnev* (1977)—both published by the Institute of International Studies.

INSTITUTE OF INTERNATIONAL STUDIES
UNIVERSITY OF CALIFORNIA, BERKELEY

215 Moses Hall   Berkeley, California 94720

CARL G. ROSBERG, *Director*

Monographs published by the Institute include:

RESEARCH SERIES

1. *The Chinese Anarchist Movement.* R.A. Scalapino and G.T. Yu. ($1.00)
7. *Birth Rates in Latin America.* O. Andrew Collver. ($2.50)
15. *Central American Economic Integration.* Stuart I. Fagan. ($2.00)
16. *The International Imperatives of Technology.* Eugene B. Skolnikoff. ($2.95)
17. *Autonomy or Dependence in Regional Integration.* P.C. Schmitter. ($1.75)
19. *Entry of New Competitors in Yugoslav Market Socialism.* S.R. Sacks. ($2.50)
20. *Political Integration in French-Speaking Africa.* Abdul A. Jalloh. ($3.50)
21. *The Desert & the Sown: Nomads in Wider Society.* Ed. C. Nelson. ($5.50)
22. *U.S.-Japanese Competition in International Markets.* J.E. Roemer. ($3.95)
23. *Political Disaffection Among British University Students.* J. Citrin and D.J. Elkins. ($2.00)
24. *Urban Inequality and Housing Policy in Tanzania.* Richard E. Stren. ($2.95)
25. *The Obsolescence of Regional Integration Theory.* Ernst B. Haas. ($4.95)
26. *The Voluntary Service Agency in Israel.* Ralph M. Kramer. ($2.00)
27. *The SOCSIM Microsimulation Program.* E. A. Hammel et al. ($4.50)
28. *Authoritarian Politics in Communist Europe.* Ed. Andrew C. Janos. ($3.95)
29. *The Anglo-Icelandic Cod War of 1972-1973.* Jeffrey A. Hart. ($2.00)
30. *Plural Societies and New States.* Robert Jackson. ($2.00)
31. *Politics of Oil Pricing in the Middle East, 1970-75.* R.C. Weisberg. ($4.95)
32. *Agricultural Policy and Performance in Zambia.* Doris J. Dodge. ($4.95)
33. *Five Classy Computer Programs.* E.A. Hammel & R.Z. Deuel. ($3.75)
34. *Housing the Urban Poor in Africa.* Richard E. Stren. ($5.95)
35. *The Russian New Right: Right-Wing Ideologies in USSR.* A. Yanov. ($5.95)
36. *Social Change in Romania, 1860-1940.* Ed. Kenneth Jowitt. ($4.50)
37. *The Leninist Response to National Dependency.* Kenneth Jowitt. ($4.95)
38. *Socialism in Sub-Saharan Africa.* Eds. C. Rosberg & T. Callaghy. ($12.95)
39. *Tanzania's Ujamaa Villages: Rural Development Strategy.* D. McHenry. ($5.95)
40. *Who Gains from Deep Ocean Mining?* I.G. Bulkley. ($3.50)
41. *Industrialization & the Nation-State in Peru.* Frits Wils. ($5.95)
42. *Ideology, Public Opinion, & Welfare Policy: Taxes and Spending in Industrialized Societies.* R.M. Coughlin. ($6.50)
43. *The Apartheid Regime: Political Power and Racial Domination.* Eds. R.M. Price and C. G. Rosberg. ($12.50)
44. *Yugoslav Economic System in the 1970s.* L.D. Tyson. ($5.50)
45. *Conflict in Chad.* Virginia Thompson & Richard Adloff. ($7.50)
46. *Conflict and Coexistence in Belgium.* Ed. Arend Lijphart. ($7.50)

47. *Changing Realities in Southern Africa.* Ed. Michael Clough. ($12.50)
48. *Nigerian Women Mobilized: Women's Political Activity in Southern Nigeria, 1900-1965.* Nina Emma Mba. ($12.95)
49. *Institutions of Rural Development for the Poor.* Ed. D. Leonard & D. Marshall. ($11.50)
50. *Politics of Women & Work in USSR & U.S.* J.C. Moses. ($9.50)
51. *Zionism and Territory.* Baruch Kimmerling. ($12.50)
52. *Soviet Subsidization of Trade with Eastern Europe.* M. Marrese & J. Vanous. ($14.50)
53. *Voluntary Efforts in Decentralized Management.* L. Ralston et al. ($9.00)
54. *Corporate State Ideologies.* C. Landauer. ($5.95)
55. *Effects of Economic Reform in Yugoslavia.* J. Burkett. ($9.50)

POLITICS OF MODERNIZATION SERIES

1. *Spanish Bureaucratic-Patrimonialism in America.* M. Sarfatti. ($2.00)
2. *Civil-Military Relations in Argentina, Chile, & Peru.* L. North. ($2.00)
9. *Modernization & Bureaucratic-Authoritarianism: Studies in South American Politics.* Guillermo O'Donnell. ($8.95)

POLICY PAPERS IN INTERNATIONAL AFFAIRS

1. *Images of Detente & the Soviet Political Order.* K. Jowitt. ($1.25)
2. *Detente After Brezhnev: Domestic Roots of Soviet Policy.* A. Yanov. ($4.50)
3. *Mature Neighbor Policy: A New Policy for Latin America.* A. Fishlow. ($3.95)
4. *Five Images of Soviet Future: Review & Synthesis.* G.W. Breslauer. ($4.50)
5. *Global Evangelism Rides Again: How to Protect Human Rights Without Really Trying.* E.B. Haas. ($2.95)
6. *Israel & Jordan: An Adversarial Partnership.* Ian Lustick. ($2.00)
7. *Political Syncretism in Italy.* Giuseppe Di Palma. ($3.95)
8. *U.S. Foreign Policy in Sub-Saharan Africa.* R.M. Price. ($4.50)
9. *East-West Technology Transfer in Perspective.* R.J. Carrick. ($5.50)
10. *NATO's Unremarked Demise.* Earl C. Ravenal. ($3.50)
11. *Toward Africanized Policy for Southern Africa.* R. Libby. ($5.50)
12. *Taiwan Relations Act & Defense of ROC.* E. Snyder et al. ($7.50)
13. *Cuba's Policy in Africa, 1959-1980.* William M. LeoGrande. ($4.50)
14. *Norway, NATO, & Forgotten Soviet Challenge.* K. Amundsen. ($2.95)
15. *Japanese Industrial Policy.* Ira Magaziner and Thomas Hout. ($6.50)
16. *Containment, Soviet Behavior, & Grand Strategy.* Robert Osgood. ($5.50)
17. *U.S.-Japanese Competition in Semiconductor Industry.* M. Borrus et al. ($7.50)
18. *Contemporary Islamic Movements in Perspective.* I. Lapidus. ($4.95)
19. *Atlantic Alliance, Nuclear Weapons, & European Attitudes.* W. Thies. ($4.50)